Critical Issues for
Student Affairs

Arthur Sandeen
Margaret Barr

Critical Issues for Student Affairs

Challenges and Opportunities

JOSSEY-BASS
A Wiley Imprint
www.josseybass.com

Published by Jossey-Bass
A Wiley Imprint
989 Market Street, San Francisco, CA 94103-1741   www.josseybass.com

Jossey-Bass books and products are available through most bookstores. To contact Jossey-Bass directly call our Customer Care Department within the U.S. at 800-956-7739, outside the U.S. at 317-572-3986, or fax 317-572-4002.

Jossey-Bass also publishes its books in a variety of electronic formats. Some content that appears in print may not be available in electronic books.

Library of Congress Cataloging-in-Publication Data
Sandeen, Arthur, 1938-
  Critical issues for student affairs : challenges and opportunities / Arthur Sandeen, Margaret Barr.— 1st ed.
     p. cm.
  Includes bibliographical references and index.
  ISBN-13: 978-0-7879-7657-6
  ISBN-10: 0-7879-7657-1
  1. Student affairs services. 2. Student affairs administrators. I. Barr, Margaret J. II. Title.
  LB2342.9.S26 2006
  378.1'97—dc22
                          2006001256

Printed in the United States of America
FIRST EDITION
HB Printing   10 9 8 7 6 5 4 3 2 1

The Jossey-Bass
Higher and Adult Education Series

Contents

Preface

What is now known as student affairs has its formal origins in the late nineteenth century. Student affairs emerged at a time of growth and change in higher education. Functions and services, once in the faculty domain, were moved to professionals whose prime responsibility was the care of students. As faculty interests changed, due to a variety of factors, circumstances required that someone be responsible for students (other than the faculty), and the roles of dean of men and dean of women were created. Those early pioneers of the profession could hardly imagine the complex roles, responsibilities, functions, and services currently provided by most student affairs organizations. Indeed, student affairs divisions and units are now part of the administration and management structure of almost every college and university in the United States. Measured against any standards, the student affairs profession has never been stronger.

Yet a number of lingering questions and issues have continued to engage the time, energy, and creativity of members of the profession, but these concerns remain unresolved. The impetus for this volume was to present critical issues that we believe must be answered by student affairs and higher education in the coming years. This specific set of issues emerged as a result of discussions based on our combined years of experience as vice presidents for student affairs and as student affairs professionals. We both believe it is critical that the student affairs profession and our colleagues in higher education carefully examine these issues and begin the process of resolving some of these concerns.

Some caveats are in order. First, we do not claim that these are the only critical issues that must be resolved by higher education and student affairs. These are the issues that we believe are most pressing and are the issues that fundamentally influence the role of student affairs within the educational enterprise. Second, we do not claim to have the answers regarding these questions. Instead in this volume, we attempt to describe the concerns and their implications and make suggestions for the profession and higher education to consider. We do not claim to have a "one-size-fits-all" answer to the questions and issues we pose. It is our hope, however, that this volume will stimulate civil discussion and debate about the nine issues discussed in this book. Some questions can be answered only on an institutional level, and the answers may be different in each institution because of the diversity of the American higher education system. Some of the questions can only be answered by individual student affairs professionals as they contemplate their role, function, purpose, and status within higher education. Some of the questions can only be answered by the total profession in careful examination of the issues and concerns that are relevant to the resolution of the issue.

Each chapter in this volume addresses one of the questions we believe are important. Chapter One focuses on identifying both common and divergent foundations for the shared profession of student affairs. This issue has been at the center of many conference discussions, journal articles, and other professional discussions. The debates have often focused on what separates the profession rather than on what unites the profession in a common core of beliefs, values, and ethics. We believe that the debate should focus on distilling the common philosophical, theoretical, and ethical constructs that unite the profession rather than assuming one point of view is more meritorious than another.

Chapter Two focuses on what is the most appropriate place for student affairs within the organizational structure of an institution of higher education. This has been a debate of long standing and has consumed time and energy of professionals and professional associations. In this chapter, the issues are examined and a new perspective is presented on the organizational placement of student affairs in the institution and the factors involved in that placement.

Chapter Three concentrates on the need for students to learn about diversity and the role of student affairs in that process. Diversity is an issue for all students enrolled in higher education and is not just a concern for underrepresented groups in the student population. What has the profession done and what can we do to make real progress on this major concern for higher education and the nation? The chapter concludes with some suggestions for consideration by the profession.

Chapter Four is linked to the concern expressed in Chapter Three. How can the student affairs profession attract and retain a diverse staff? The meaning of a diverse staff is explored as well as methods to attain staff diversity. The chapter concludes with some ideas to move this agenda forward to resolution.

Funding is a major issue for higher education, in general, and student affairs in particular. Chapter Five focuses on funding for student affairs and the implications of funding decisions. What are the barriers to receiving sound financial support for programs and services provided by student affairs? What are the problems and pitfalls associated with some funding sources? What is the role of student affairs in development of institutional budget priorities and funding methods? This chapter poses issues that the senior management in student affairs must come to grips with as fiscal resources become more restricted, and it makes suggestions for consideration by the profession.

There has been great growth in non-traditional educational settings, and many college students are using such programs as a prime educational experience. Chapter Six focuses on the obligations of student affairs organizations to students studying via technology, on branch campuses, in centers, in study abroad programs, and in externships, internships, and cooperative education programs. As a profession, we have not been central to the development of such programs and services. We believe that the role of student affairs in this arena must be redefined in the future, and we make some suggestions for consideration in that discussion.

Assessment has been part of the lexicon of higher education for some time. Outcomes measures are being required by legislative bodies and accrediting groups. Student affairs, however, has not been a leading partner in the assessment efforts on most campuses. The calls for assessment and outcomes for higher education are not likely to diminish in the years ahead. Chapter Seven focuses on the assessment question and the potential role of student affairs in such efforts, and it provides some suggestions for consideration by the profession and professional associations.

In Chapter Eight, the complex and difficult question of who has responsibility for the lives of students is discussed. Legal requirements, institutional missions, parental expectations, chronic psychological problems of students, and student behaviors require both the profession and institutions to answer this fundamental question. In this chapter, the complexity of the issues is presented, along with some suggestions to begin dialogue on this complex issue.

In Chapter Nine, the question of how professional associations should serve the profession is discussed. The astonishing proliferation of professional associations is examined, and the intended and unintended consequences of such growth are explored. Key questions are presented for consideration by the profession as a whole and by the many subgroups that comprise student affairs.

It would be presumptuous of us to claim that we have the answers to these complex and difficult questions. We do, however, posit these issues for consideration by professionals and the profession. It is hoped that the volume will be useful to current student affairs professionals engaged in program review, long-range planning, and unit evaluation. We believe that this volume will provide information and perspectives to sitting vice presidents and deans as they attempt to answer these questions on their own campuses and to communicate with other institutional leadership about these issues. The volume will be helpful to the leadership of the many professional organizations serving student affairs as they plan their programs, services, and agendas for the future. It also will be useful to students in graduate education programs at both the master's and doctoral levels as they learn about the profession they have chosen.

Finally, we believe that these issues have far-reaching implications for the future of student affairs and higher education. We urge that they not be ignored and that intentional efforts be made to resolve the issues presented here through discussion and debate on the individual campuses within the community of higher education and professional associations and by individual professionals.

Our hope is that this volume provides a positive stimulus for such discussions, debates, and ultimate decisions. Both of us have great faith in the wisdom, ethics, energy, passion, compassion, and skills of our student affairs colleagues as they engage in this important process. They have taught us a great deal, enriched our professional and personal lives, engaged us in fascinating issues, and helped us grow and develop as professionals. For their wisdom and friendship, we are grateful. This volume would not have been possible without the knowledge gained and the lessons learned from our professional friends and colleagues.

Arthur Sandeen
Professor of Higher Education
(Retired)
Vice President for Student
Affairs Emeritus
University of Florida

Margaret Barr
Professor Emeritus of Education
and Social Policy
Former Vice President for
Student Affairs (Retired)
Northwestern University

About the Authors

Arthur Sandeen earned his bachelor's degree in religion and psychology in 1960 from Miami University in Oxford, Ohio; his master's degree in college student personnel administration from Michigan State University in 1962; and his doctorate from Michigan State in 1965 in administration and higher education. In 1982, he was a Fulbright Scholar in West Germany and in 1984 completed the Institute for Educational Management Program at Harvard University.

Sandeen served as a head resident adviser and coordinator of freshman orientation at Michigan State from 1962 to 1965 and as associate director of residence hall programs (1965–1967) at Michigan State. He then served as associate dean of students and assistant professor of higher education at Iowa State University (1967–1969), and from 1969 to 1973, he served as dean of students and associate professor of higher education at Iowa State University. In 1973, he was appointed vice president for student affairs and professor of higher education at the University of Florida and served in that position until August 1999. He continued to serve as professor of higher education at the University of Florida until his retirement in 2004.

He was elected president of the National Association of Student Personnel Administrators (NASPA) in 1977 and chaired the committee that wrote the report "A Perspective on Student Affairs," commemorating the fiftieth anniversary of the *Student Personnel Point of View*. He received the Fred Turner Award in 1982 for contributions to NASPA, the Scott Goodnight Award (1990) for outstanding performance as a dean, and the Contribution to Literature and Research Award from NASPA (2000). In 2001, at the invitation of the Asian-Pacific Student Services Association, he conducted a student affairs institute in Hong Kong.

Sandeen is the author of numerous articles and book chapters and has written *Undergraduate Education: Conflict and Change* (1976), *The Chief Student Affairs Officer: Leader, Manager, Mediator, Educator* (1991), *Improving Student Affairs Administration* (2000), *Making A Difference: Profiles of Outstanding Student Affairs Leaders* (2001), and *Enhancing Student Engagement on Campus* (2003).

He is married to Sue Swezey Sandeen. They have two daughters and five grandchildren.

Margaret Barr served as vice president for student affairs at Northwestern University from October 1992 until July 2000 when she retired. She currently is professor emeritus in the School of Education and Social Policy at Northwestern. She served as vice chancellor for student affairs at Texas Christian University (1985–1992) and as vice president for student affairs at Northern Illinois University (1982–1985). She previously served as assistant vice president for student affairs at Northern Illinois University (1980–1982), associate dean of students at the University of Texas at Austin (1979–1980), and assistant dean of students at the University of Texas at Austin (1971–1979). Prior to that time, she served in various student affairs positions at Trenton State College and the State University of New York at Binghamton.

She has been active in National Association of Student Personnel Administrators (NASPA), including service as director of the Richard F. Stevens Institute for Chief Student Affairs Officers (1989, 1990), was president of the NASPA Foundation Board, and was a member of the committee that wrote "A Perspective on

Student Affairs." Barr received the NASPA Outstanding Contribution to Literature and Research (1986) and the NASPA Outstanding Contribution to Higher Education Award (2000).

She also was active in the American College Personnel Association (ACPA), serving as president (1983–1984). She was named a Senior Scholar (1986–1991), and received the Professional Service Award (1991) and the Contribution to Knowledge Award (1990) from ACPA.

She is the author or editor of *An Academic Manager's Guide to Budgets and Financial Management* (2002), *A Handbook for Student Affairs Administration* (1993), senior editor of the second edition of *A Handbook for Student Affairs Administration* (2000) with M. Desler, coeditor of *New Futures for Student Affairs* with M. L. Upcraft (1990), *Student Services and the Law* (1988), and *Developing Effective Student Services Programs* with L. Keating (1985). In addition, she served as editor-in-chief of the monograph series *New Directions for Student Services* (1986–1998).

Barr received a bachelor's degree in elementary education from the State University College at Buffalo (1961), a master's degree in college student personnel from Southern Illinois University-Carbondale (1963), and a doctorate in educational administration from the University of Texas at Austin (1980). She was a Fulbright Scholar in Germany in 1986.

What Is the Foundation
of Student Affairs?

Everyone knows that any building needs a strong foundation. Whether it is a small cottage or an immense skyscraper, each building must have a foundation designed to support the structure through years of inclement weather, heavy use, and natural disasters. Buildings without strong foundations will collapse and fall when faced with both anticipated and unanticipated stresses and strains. A strong foundation, however, can support a structure through time and is essential to the longevity and integrity of the building.

Professions also are built on foundations, although such foundations are not made with bricks, mortar, reinforcing rods, and pylons. The foundation of any profession is formed from a shared philosophy about what needs to be done, a shared understanding of the theoretical constructs that inform the practice of the profession, the application of the accumulated knowledge of the members to the tasks that need to be accomplished, and the ability of the practitioners of the profession to effectively link their theoretical knowledge, practical wisdom, and skills to larger organizations and society. Finally, a profession articulates standards by which its performance can be judged by those who are not members of the profession.

For example, consider the profession of medicine. It is a profession that has a shared philosophy, embodied in the Hippocratic Oath, of what needs to be done. Medicine also clearly has a vast

number of theoretical constructs regarding how the human body
works, how disease manifests itself, how problems can be corrected,
and how new cures might occur. Many of these theories have been
tested, some are just evolving, and others have been discarded
through careful review and rigorous examination in the laboratory
and clinical trials. Medicine is not just a set of theories; it is characterized by skilled practitioners who are applying their accumulated knowledge of the field to the problem at hand in working with
patients. Individual medical practitioners do not stand alone; they
are linked with one another through professional organizations and
a web of other caregivers. They are supported in their endeavors
through a vast array of medical institutions. Finally, medicine pro-
mulgates and enforces standards, has established accreditation
guidelines, has sanctions, and has a code of ethics. Although this
may be a simplistic analysis of the medical profession, it provides an
instructive framework for an examination of the profession of student affairs and the foundations that support that work.

Strong foundations do not occur by accident. They are the result
of hard work, careful planning, examination of strengths and weaknesses, and provision of needed reinforcement at critical times. Student affairs, as a profession, has been characterized by internal
debate regarding the "true" foundations of the profession. For some,
the roots of the profession are in counseling and counseling theories; for others, the foundation of the profession is student development theory and practice; and for still others, the appropriate
foundation for student affairs is based on organizational theory,
administration, and management. With such divergent points of
view within the profession, the foundation can at times feel like it is
built on quicksand. The debate can become heated and is ultimately
self-defeating for both practitioners and the profession. This chapter presents the point of view that although there are differences
between and among student affairs professionals, there is a common
foundation that supports the work of the profession. Over time,
several key concepts have been embedded in both philosophical

statements and theoretical constructs. The chapter will present a discussion of the philosophical and theoretical building blocks that provide a common foundation for student affairs practice. Included will be key references to documents that have helped shape the profession to the present time. The chapter will conclude with a discussion of the implications of this issue for graduate preparation programs and provide recommendations regarding the future of the foundation of student affairs.

Philosophical Foundations

"Student affairs is largely an American higher education invention" (Rhatigan, 2000, p. 5). The breadth and diversity of institutions of higher education in the United States are unique in the world. Institutions differ in terms of mission, size, type, affiliations, and scope. In addition, American students are among the most heterogeneous in the world, reflecting a wide range of backgrounds and purposes for attending institutions of higher education. The diversity of American higher education did not occur by accident. Higher education, in the United States, grew and changed to reflect the massive changes occurring in the greater American society, including, but not limited to, the abolishment of slavery, the emancipation of women, the civil rights movement, overseas conflicts, wars, and other factors. Readers are urged to review Thelin (2003), Rhatigan (2000), Brubacher and Rudy (1976), and Rudolph (1965) for a full discussion of the factors and issues that provide the context for the development of higher education and student affairs.

Student affairs also reflects the diverse nature of American higher education. Nuss reminds us, however, that two important concepts have characterized student affairs from the advent of the early deans of men and women to the present day, saying in part that "as you consider the history of student affairs, please note two enduring and distinctive concepts. The first is the profession's consistent and persistent commitment to the development of the whole person. In spite of the dramatic changes that have occurred in higher education, the profession's adherence to this fundamental principle should not be overlooked or underestimated. Second, student affairs was originally founded to support the academic mission of the college, and one of the characteristic strengths of American higher education is the diversity among the missions of these institutions" (Nuss, 2003, pp. 65–66).

The Pioneers

The early deans of women and deans of men were the true pioneers of the profession of student affairs. Rhatigan (2000) notes that without a prior history, definitive job descriptions, or set agendas, these men and women developed a strategy and an agenda for their work with students. In contrast to professionals today, all they had were their own experiences, education, values, personal skills, and leadership abilities (p. 8). It is clear, however, that these early pioneers laid the first foundation stones for the profession of student affairs. Even though time and history obscure much of what they did, these individuals made a difference. Whether their focus was on standards, or vocational development of students, or discipline, their professional activities clearly reflected both adherence to the concept of developing the whole person and supporting the unique mission of each institution where they served.

The work of these early pioneers, and those who came immediately after them, was informed by a variety of theories and perspectives emanating from sociology, psychology, educational psychology, vocational guidance, assessment, and mental health. The work of Scott, Strong, Thorndike, Watson, and others influenced the growing profession of student affairs. Often the overarching framework that led the efforts of these individuals was an acceptance of humanism as a guiding point of view (Rhatigan, 2000). This humanistic orientation provided a framework for much discussion and debate. One result was the 1937 document *The Student Personnel Point of View,* commissioned and approved by the American Council on Education (ACE).

The Student Personnel Point of View, 1937

This document has been a critical part of the foundation for student affairs. Although certainly not perfect, and reflecting the times in which it was written, the document focuses attention on the two elements identified by Nuss (2003): commitment to the development of the whole person and support of the mission of the institution. The document states in part that "personnel work is not new. Personnel officers have been appointed throughout the colleges and universities of this country to undertake a number of educational responsibilities which were once entirely assumed by teaching members of the faculty. They have also, because of the expansion of educational functions, developed a number of student personnel services which have but recently been stressed. The philosophy behind their works, however, is as old as education itself" (p. 51). This statement is a powerful affirmation of the role of student affairs within higher education and the philosophical underpinnings of the field.

The statement goes on to list a number of functions that should be of concern to the student affairs profession. In addition, it emphasizes the need to coordinate the work of student affairs within the institution, including coordination with the faculty and business administration. Research is an important agenda item from the 1937 statement and remains a current concern for the profession today. The enduring nature of these recommendations and suggestions make the 1937 statement one of the keystones of the foundation of the current work of student affairs.

After the upheaval of World War II, the subsequent enrollment surge of veterans, and the resulting expansion of the higher education enterprise, ACE commissioned another statement in 1949 on *The Student Personnel Point of View*.

The Student Personnel Point of View, 1949

The 1949 statement expanded the philosophy of higher education expressed in *The Student Personnel Point of View* (American Council on Education, 1937) to include emphasis on preparing citizens for

roles in public affairs and addressing social problems in a democratic society, and it forecasted the need for increased emphasis on
aiding students with information focused on international understanding and cooperation. The statement reaffirms the commitment
of student affairs to the development of the whole person, saying in
part that:

> The student personnel movement constitutes one of the
> most important efforts of American educators, to treat
> college and university students as individuals, rather
> than as entities on an impersonal roster. The movement,
> at the same time, expresses awareness of the significance
> of student group life in its manifold expressions from
> student residences to student mores, from problems of
> admission to problems of job placement. It has devel-
> oped as the division of college and university adminis-
> tration concerned with students individually and in
> groups. In a real sense, this part of modern higher edu-
> cation is an individualized application of the research
> and clinical findings of modern psychology, sociology,
> cultural anthropology, and education to the task of aid-
> ing students to develop fully in the college environment
> [ACE, 1949, p. 24].

This part of the statement clearly recognizes the organizational
role assumed by student affairs, the specialization needed within
student affairs, and the multiplicity of the theoretical constructs
that inform the professional practice of student affairs. For these reasons alone, this document should be considered another keystone
in building the foundation of student affairs. Although the 1949
statement also reflects the issues and the language of the time in
which it was written, it is inclusive and does not create an either-
or approach to how student affairs professionals should approach
their work.

A Perspective on Student Affairs

On the fiftieth anniversary of the 1939 publication of *The Student Personnel Point of View*, the National Association of Student Personnel Administrators (NASPA) issued the document *A Perspective on Student Affairs* (1989). It focused on the assumptions and beliefs that shape the work of student affairs. Essentially, these assumptions and beliefs are statements of the philosophy that guides the work of student affairs. The document clearly states that "no one of these assumptions and beliefs is unique to student affairs. Indeed, they are held by many others in higher education. It is the combination of these assumptions and beliefs that is distinctive. Together, they define the special contribution of student affairs" (National Association of Student Personnel Administrators, 1989, p. 11).

The statement goes on to affirm the preeminence of the academic mission of the institution, the unique, whole nature of the student and how all their experiences influence learning. In addition, the statement focuses on the institutional environment and the value of the many communities contained therein. Finally, the statement concludes by honoring the paradoxical nature of the work of student affairs, saying in part that "as a partner in the educational enterprise, student affairs enhances and supports the academic mission. In addition, student affairs professionals must advocate for the common good and champion the rights of the individual, encourage intelligent risk-taking and set limits on behavior; encourage independent thought and teach interdependent behavior" (National Association of Student Personnel Administrators, 1989, p. 19). This is a challenging but essential set of tasks undergirded by a foundation that emphasizes both the whole student and the mission of the institution.

Enduring Principles and Values

Woodard, Love, and Komives (2000) examined these three statements and other works, including *The Student Learning Imperative* (ACPA, 1994) and *Good Practices in Student Affairs* (Blimling,

Whitt, and Associates, 1999). Their analysis resulted in the identification of a set of enduring values that have held true through time and embody the ideals of the student affairs profession. They indicate that all of these works, and others, hold a set of common beliefs rooted in the dignity, uniqueness, potential, and worth of each person and a strong belief in the development of the whole person. In addition, they found agreement in these statements that the "mission of student affairs flows from the mission of the institution" (p. 21). They also identified concurrence among the documents that they studied on a set of beliefs regarding learning occurring in diverse places and in diverse ways and that students are ultimately responsible for their own learning and behavior. Another set of beliefs identified by Woodard, Love, and Komives focused on civil discourse, communication, and diverse communities where assumptions and beliefs should be examined and questioned (p. 21). In addition, a focus is given to the administrative and management aspects of student affairs as underlying concepts that support the profession (p. 22). This perspective regarding the powerful potential role of student affairs within the learning community challenges the profession in profound and meaningful ways.

Ethics

The ethical dimensions of the work of student affairs are certainly one of the cornerstones of the profession. Both the American College Personnel Association (ACPA) and National Association of Student Personnel Administrators (NASPA) have ethical statements that outline the duties and responsibilities for the ethical behavior of professionals. The work of Karen Kitchener (1985) provided a strong direction for the student affairs profession when she articulated five simple but powerful ethical principles for student affairs: respecting autonomy, doing no harm, helping others, being just, and being trustworthy. Those ethical principles can of course come into conflict with one another in the daily practice of student affairs, but they provide one of the strong foundations for further exploration of ethical principles as professionals work with individual students, student groups, and institutions. The works of Brown (1985), Canon (1985, 1993), Fried (1995, 2000), and Meara, Schmidt, and Day (1996) have all advanced the ethical awareness of the student affairs profession.

Among the greatest skills of a student affairs administrator is balancing the individual rights of students and the common good of the educational enterprise. Understanding and applying ethical principles in daily decisions is an essential cornerstone of effective student affairs practice.

There has been consistency over time regarding the philosophy that guides the work of student affairs. Although organizational structures may vary across institutions, and the emphasis of the work of student affairs may differ from institution to institution, the profession has embraced the notion of both fostering the development of the whole student and providing service and support to the academic mission of the institution. At times, the profession has had internal debates on what the emphasis should be in the work of student affairs. Is it management or counseling? Is it student development or administration? Is the work of student affairs primary or secondary within the institution? Those debates have turned the focus of the profession inward, instead of on the students and institutions served by the profession.

Transitional Works

Four works, labeled *transitional* for lack of a better term, have profoundly influenced the work of student affairs whether the current group of practitioners realizes it or not. The first was presented by insiders in student affairs, Esther Lloyd-Jones and her colleague, M. R. Smith (1954). A second contribution was made by a psychologist, Nevitt Sanford, in 1962, as he and his associates reported on a massive study of American higher education. The third was the publication by Ernest Boyer (1990), a leader in higher education but not from student affairs. The fourth was written by a senior student affairs officer, Gregory Blimling, and a faculty member, Elizabeth Whitt (1999). All have profoundly influenced the philosophical foundation of the profession of student affairs.

Student Personnel Work as Deeper Teaching

This book, written in 1954, provided yet another foundational building block for the work of student affairs. Lloyd-Jones and Smith stated a set of common beliefs that characterized professionals working in student affairs. This philosophy affirms the worth of the individual and states in part that "the common good can be promoted best by helping each individual to develop to the utmost in accordance with his abilities . . . the belief in the equal dignity of thinking and feeling and working; that these aspects are inseparable. Personnel work is interested in the *whole* person" (p. 5). The authors go on to say that for the student, "A stimulating and rich environment provides for the explanation of resources (relationships, who and what he is); and for the accomplishment of the developmental tasks appropriate for his age level" (p. 5). The influence of the person-environment interaction described in this volume and the developmental tasks were indeed the precursors for a number of theoretical constructs that inform the professional tasks of student affairs today.

The American College

During the 1950s and the 1960s, Nevitt Sanford and his associates conducted a major study of higher education in the United States. Two published works resulted from this study and contributed to the understanding of the collegiate experience of students and the roles and challenges faced by faculty and staff within those institutions. Focused on traditional age college students, who were the majority of those enrolled in the eras studied, *The American College* (Sanford, 1962) highlighted the effects of the collegiate experience on the total growth and development of students. It was followed by *Where Colleges Fail* (1967).

Both of these volumes reinforced the notion of the educ
the whole person through both academic study and personal deve
opment. Sanford was both a critic and a supporter of higher education. Perhaps his greatest contribution was in describing what
occurred within the collegiate environments while placing
that description into a developmental framework.

Campus Life: In Search of Community

In 1990, Ernest Boyer helped all of higher education, and most particularly student affairs, understand the influence of communities in
helping both the institution and individual students. He articulated
characteristics of positive communities that assist with learning,
growth, and development and reflect the principles of sound education. His six descriptors of positive educational communities have
had a powerful influence on later works, both philosophical and theoretical, that have affected student affairs. He indicated that a learning community, such as a college or university, should be purposeful,
open, just, disciplined, caring, and celebrative (1990). The explanation of these deceptively simple characteristics has had far-reaching
implications for contemporary and future student affairs professionals. For example, the report describes a disciplined community as "a
place where individuals accept their obligations to the group and
well-defined governance procedures guide behavior for the common
good" (p. 37). Or consider the statement that a just community
rejects prejudice and affirms diversity in all aspects of the community and "is a place where diversity is aggressively pursued" (p. 35).
Strands of each of the notions of collegiate communities, articulated
by Boyer, can be found in many contemporary discussions within
higher education and student affairs. Boyer's work had the potential to
help each professional focus on the individual, groups of students, and
thus all the parts of the institutional community. His work provided
a stronger voice for the work of some of the early theorists in person-
environment interaction, including, but not limited to, Banning
(1978), Parker (1978), and Hurst, Morrill, and Oetting (1980).

Principles of Good Practice in Student Affairs

Written by Blimling and Whitt and their associates (1999), the work provides seven principles that underpin the work of student affairs. These principles were articulated in a joint statement issued by ACPA and NASPA, *Principles of Good Practice in Student Affairs* (1997). Blimling and Whitt, however, provide a means to translate those principles into the daily work of student affairs. The principles are stated differently but are not new—they are grounded in the notions of development of the whole person and support of the institutional mission, which are foundational concepts of student affairs. The principles state that good practice in student affairs accomplishes the following: engages students in active learning, helps students develop coherent values and ethical standards, sets and communicates high expectations for learning, uses systematic inquiry to improve student and institutional performance, uses resources effectively to achieve institutional missions and goals, forges educational partnerships that enhance student learning, and builds supportive and inclusive communities (1999, pp. 14–20). The great value of this work is helping professionals understand the link between what they do on a daily basis with the learning and development of student and institutional goals.

All of these works did not arise by chance. Each referenced statement and publication was informed by the work of an eclectic group of theorists who both enhanced the understanding of the development of students and student groups and the organization of the higher education enterprise.

Theoretical Foundations

The function of theory is to describe, explain, and predict (Hoy and Miskel, 1978). Theories of assistance to student affairs practitioners come from a wide variety of disciplines, including psychology, sociol d education. Two theory groups are important to student affairs. t is a group of theories focused on the growth and development of students and specific subgroups within the student cadre. The second is research that describes and explains organizations and the application of organizational theory to higher education.

A compendium of the research on the effects of the collegiate experience on students was compiled by Pascarella and Terenzini (1991, 2005) and provides a useful framework to identify the first set of theoretical foundations for the work of student affairs. Their work was preceded by volumes by Feldman and Newcomb (1969), Chickering (1969, 1981), Astin (1977), Bowen (1979), Pace (1979), and others, but Pascarella and Terenzini presented a classification system for pertinent research that is a useful way to organize a vast amount of material. Space does not permit a full discussion of each of these theoretical constructs, but it should be noted that each theory set has contributed to the foundation of student affairs in fundamental and profound ways.

Developmental Theories of Student Change

"Developmental theories and models seek to identify the dimensions and structure of growth in college students and to explain the dynamics by which growth occurs" (Pascarella and Terenzini, 1991, p. 18). Four larger groups comprise the cluster of developmental theories of student change.

Psychosocial Theories

This set of theories involves the mastery of developmental tasks that vary with the individual's age and developmental status and the rate of mastery of those tasks. Erikson (1959) profoundly influenced the development of psychosocial theories. His concepts are that biological and psychological development is sequential, does not occur in isolation, and is influenced by the environment of the person. Further he posited that providing challenge and support to those facing developmental tasks or crises is extremely important. Finally, he stated that the dominant developmental task for traditional age college students, and other people of that same age, is identity formation.

referencing both the work of Erikson and Sanford, Chickering presented seven vectors of development that differ from stages in that they have both direction and force. The vectors he identified are achieving competence, managing emotions, developing autonomy, establishing identity, freeing interpersonal relationships, developing purpose, and developing integrity (Chickering, 1969). In 1993, Chickering and Reisser reexamined the vectors of development and strengthened the concepts by placing additional emphasis on the relationship between autonomy, independence, and intimacy and the complexity of those interactions. Further they asserted that the capstone of autonomy was interdependence (Chickering and Reisser, 1993).

Douglas Heath (1968, 1978) presented a complex maturity model that differed from other developmental theories in that it focused on five dimensions of maturation, where movement toward maturation occurs within the self-systems of the person. Heath's work also is distinguished by its emphasis on relating the model to the tenets of a liberal education.

Other theorists also have contributed to the understanding of students from a psychosocial perspective, including, but not limited to, the following. Marcia (1966) posited a model of ego identity status. Cross's model of black identity formation (1985) and Helms's work (1990), which seeks to describe the developmental process whereby the individual becomes "black," also have made enormous contributions to an understanding of African-American students. The works of Cuyjet (1997), Howard-Hamilton (1997), and Wright (1987) have aided practitioners in translating the emerging theoretical perspectives about the development of African American students into practice.

Cognitive-Structural Theories

Perry's theory of intellectual and ethical development (1970, 1981) led the way in developing an understanding of how individuals construe knowledge, value, and responsibility. His theory is a complex stage model and was based on a study of Harvard men. Kohlberg's work (1969) also is a stage theory, focused more narrowly on what must happen within the individual before moral choices and judgments are made. Much of Kohlberg's work focused on male populations.

Gilligan's model of a different voice (1977) identified differences between men and women, when applying Kohlberg's model. It states that Kohlberg's model does not accurately apply to women regarding their sense of self and the basis of their moral reasoning. Gilligan goes on to state that one theory of moral development is not "right" and another "wrong," but they are different perspectives on the same phenomena.

Kitchener and King (1981) have developed a reflective judgment model. Loevinger (1976) posits a theory of ego development. Both are stage models and have contributed to the understanding of the profession on how students grow, mature, develop, and make choices in life.

Typological Models

This set of models categorizes people into groups based on the distinctive characteristics that distinguish one group from another. These typological models describe stability in the differences of individuals over time. More descriptive in nature, these models do not attempt to explain the characteristics and processes of individual change but instead are helpful in focusing on the differences among students and how different students may react differently to the same perceived situation.

The Myers-Briggs Typology is perhaps the best known of these typological models and is used on many college campuses and organizations to determine the type of approach individuals take to problem solving and social interaction (Myers, 1980). Since the advent of the Myers-Briggs, a number of other theories related to the typology of persons have surfaced, but research has been scanty on those emerging theories.

Person-Environment Interaction Models

As noted earlier, person-environment interaction models are important to the foundation of student affairs. Such theories do not attempt to explain and predict the development of the individual but focus instead on the environment and how, through interaction, it influences the individual. Barker's work (1968) is the most fully developed theory of person-environment interaction.

Holland's work (1966, 1985) on vocational choice is among the best known of this group of theories and also blends some typological characteristics and psychosocial theories. Holland's work is differentiated by his conclusion that it is the interaction of the personality of the individual and the environment in which that person finds him- or herself that determines behavior. When there is congruence between the individual and the environment, there is a great likelihood of stability. When the individual experiences inconsistencies, change occurs within the individual or the individual leaves the environment.

The work of Moos (1979) provided a significant contribution when he applied person-environmental interaction theories to the work of higher education. Pace and Stern (1958) developed an environmental press model that is still in use today. Banning (1978) provided helpful translation of this set of theories to the work of student affairs.

The landmark work *Involving Colleges* (Kuh, Schuh and Whitt, 1991) helped the profession better understand what factors, including practices and policies, influence the learning, growth, and development of students in general and individual students in particular. Their observations and descriptions of many institutions over time have informed student affairs practitioners and institutions of strategies that are successful in helping students achieve educational goals.

Newest Theories

The greatest number of theoretical advancements in recent years have focused on theories about student subpopulations, including women, men, African Americans, Asian Americans, Latinos, and

Native Americans and also on sexual orientation. Because these are the populations that are growing most rapidly in American higher education, these theories as they are tested and modeled should not be excluded from the foundation of student affairs. Theories related to women and African Americans have received the most attention, but recent work points to theories of student change and development related to other ethnic groups and sexual orientation. Space does not permit a full discussion of all of these theories, but they are important additions to the foundation of student affairs. The reader is referred to several volumes that can be useful to understand this growing and important branch of theory.

Identity Development of Diverse Populations: Implications for Teaching and Administration in Higher Education (2003) by Torres, Howard-Hamilton, and Cooper provides an excellent overview of identity development theories related to race, ethnicity, gender, and sexual orientation. It discusses the implications of those theoretical developments to administration and provides a broad overview for the student affairs administrators.

In *Working with Asian American College Students* (2003) McEwen, Kodama, Alvarez, Lee, and Liang provide both theoretical constructs and practical advice on working with Asian American students. The authors propose a model for Asian American student development and translate that model into practical ideas for student affairs administrators.

Anna Ortiz and her colleagues (2004) provide insight in *Addressing the Unique Needs of Latino American Students* by aiding practitioners in understanding the differences between and among Latino students as well as the role cultural identity plays in their growth and development. The volume includes a number of practical suggestions for putting these insights to work for student success.

Fox, Lowe, and McClellan (2005) provide understanding of the Native American student experience and help practitioners understand a different approach to learning and community. The role of the tribe and family in the success of students is explored in detail, as a different cultural approach to growth and development is presented.

These are but a few of the new voices that are contributing to the foundation of student affairs theory. Their voices must be included and the foundation of student development theories expanded if student affairs is to serve the new students entering our campuses.

Organizational Theories

Student affairs, as a profession, has paid much more attention to the individual growth and development of students than to the larger organization of higher education, where the profession must function effectively in order to succeed. Most of the debate, within the profession, has focused on organizational structures, reporting relationships, financial concerns, and other matters (see other chapters in this volume) rather than on understanding the complex dynamics of an institution of higher education.

Kuh (1989) identified four models of organizations that can influence the work of student affairs: the rational model, the bureaucratic model, the collegial model, and the political model. It is a useful way to discuss organizational theory and the influence those theories can have on the work of student affairs.

Rational Model

Kuh (2003) indicates that the rational model for organizations is appealing because it emphasizes qualities valued in the academy: fairness and objectivity in decision making, deliberate and purposeful action, and predictable outcomes. It is limited, however, because it makes an assumption that everyone in the organization shares the same goals, and the model relies on formalized regulations and supervision within the organization. In *Involving Colleges*, cited earlier in this chapter, Kuh, Schuh, Whitt, and their associates (1991) described several institutions where such a rational model exists. They are small and single focused (primarily on liberal education) and may be church related. Ambler (2000) indicates, however, that because it assumes such a shared mission and goals, it has limitations in its application to large and complex institutions and systems.

Bureaucratic Model

Max Weber (1947) developed an organizational model that puts priority on hierarchical power, limits on authority, specialization of functions, technical competence, an impersonal orientation, efficiency, and standard operating procedures. The bureaucratic model is evident in colleges and universities, but it does not characterize the entire organization of the institution. Even though institutions may have standard operating procedures and organizational charts, pure reason and standard procedures do not work throughout the academy. For example, it is not unusual in a highly competitive Division I institution to have the salary of the head football or basketball coach exceed the salary of the provost or highest-paid faculty member. If the purpose of higher education is academic, such compensation packages clearly are not rational.

Further, Kuh indicates, "Some of the traditions of the academy, such as academic freedom and collegial governance, are incompatible with many bureaucratic principles of organizing" (1989, p. 217). Bureaucratic rules are a source of frustration for many student affairs administrators, who are used to dealing with the unexpected and unpredictable elements of the collegiate experience. Such rules can, however, provide a screening function for an administrator to reduce levels of interpersonal tension regarding a decision. Reliance on bureaucratic rules also can have unanticipated outcomes because such rules rely on minimal standards, and if they are constantly employed by an administrator, the minimums can become the maximum expectation for performance. In addition, the bureaucratic model of organizations neglects the informal organization—an organization can only be really understood if there is awareness of both the formal and informal patterns of communication and decision making within the organization. The bureaucratic model of organizations does not account for such variability.

Collegial Model

In a collegial model, there is an assumption of common goals and priorities within the institution or organization. This model is predicated on the assumption that participatory governance is the most appropriate way to pursue and meet institutional goals (Chaffee, 1983) and that assumption is reflected in all levels of the organization.

The tripartite assemblies that grew out of the campus unrest of the sixties are examples of the collegial model at work. Representatives of faculty, staff, and students met regularly to discuss issues and concerns common to everyone in the institution. The assumption was made that no matter what the topic, everyone had a right to state an opinion, and civil discourse could occur that would eventually end in a decision embraced by all.

Unionization, faculty loyalty to their disciplines rather than the institution, and a sense that the process was not really collegial at all undermined this model on many campuses. Changes in the external environment, including legal mandates for certain accommodations, practices, and policies resulted, at times, in the collegial model being ineffective. Many agendas could not be completely resolved within the context of the academy. In addition, the assumption of collegiality does not address the issues of conflict resolution within a campus community and does not provide methods for resolution of deeply held positions and philosophies by groups within the institution. The utility of the collegial model is questioned by many, for it presents an ideal rather than the reality of decision making, power and authority, and legal constraints faced by most higher education institutions.

Political Model

Kantor and Stein (1979) described politicized organizations as those existing under conditions where "environments press or need to be managed, when stakeholders are activated, when interests are strong" (p. 303). Their description is a fair and accurate one of most institutions of higher education. A political view of higher education challenges the assumptions of other models.

Stakeholders in higher education come from both without and within the institution, and each stakeholder group has an agenda. Conflicts will invariably arise between and among stakeholder groups. For example, students may see a need for a new academic program, but that identified need is not a priority for the faculty. Or staff members feel they are not receiving adequate compensation, but parents and students want money spent on new recreational facilities. The list of potential and real conflicts between stakeholder groups within higher education is long and complex and the conflicts are not easily resolved.

Power becomes an important commodity in politicized organizations, and there are many forms of power. Appleton (1991) describes several types of power that can be exercised within an organization: positional power, referent power, coercion, personal influence, and expert power. The use of power in decision making is a cornerstone of the political view of organizations. Moore (2000) also describes other aspects of political organization that are particularly applicable to student affairs. He states, in part, that there are unique aspects of institutions of higher education that shape the political environment within the institution: goal diffusion, uncertainty of means to accomplish goals, dual control, structural uniqueness, limits of leadership, and the unique organizational culture of each institution.

Since Kantor and Stein (1979) described politicized organizations, a great many changes have occurred to increase politicization of institutions of higher education. For example, technology brings conflicts and debates that were once internal to the institution into the purview of others through Web pages, e-mail, and blogs. Funding has become more restricted and priorities of institutions have shifted and changed. These factors and others have contributed to greater political stresses within higher education. Still, many in student affairs are not comfortable with the notion that colleges and universities are political organizations and that conflict might be resolved through political means rather than rational discourse and collegiality.

Other Models

A number of other theories and models also are useful in understanding the internal dynamics of any college or university organization.

Organizational Culture

Schein is particularly helpful in understanding and applying the theory of organizational cultures. He states in part that "the organizations that have survived and made important transitions over many decades seem to have a cultural core that was fundamentally functional—a commitment to learning and change; a commitment to people and all of the stakeholders in the organizations including customers, employees, suppliers and stockholders and a commitment to building a healthy, flexible organization in the first place" (Schein, 1992, p. 62). Although discussing business and industry, his words have direct application to higher education and student affairs. This view of organizations is less precise than some other perspectives, but it is a useful tool for the practitioner in higher education.

Organized Anarchy

Kuh (2003) indicates that the organized anarchy view of organizations "was developed specifically to describe six characteristics peculiar to colleges and universities" (p. 277). Referencing Baldridge (1971) and Cohen and Marsh (1972), Kuh describes these unique characteristics as ambiguity, conflicting goals, unclear technology, fluid participation, a highly educated workforce, and clients who participate in the governance of the institution. Any budget cycle at any institution reveals the issues of ambiguity and conflicting goals. For example, many worthy ideas are forwarded, but only a few can be funded due to scarce resources. Loose coupling refers to the strength of the relationships between and among parts of the organization. Rather than being tightly controlled interactions, as described in other organizational theories, relationships between offices and agencies are random and are thoughtfully encouraged. To illustrate, recently an admissions officer indicated that she was unsure that her predictions regarding the size of the freshman class were accurate. Her uncertainty arose because the weekly report on housing applications and deposits forwarded by residence life showed far fewer applications for housing than might be expected at a specific point in time. When she inquired, however, the applications were in but had not been processed because a key staff member was out of the office. Her worry was for nothing and the residence life staff had been unaware that their delay in processing might have an influence on any other part of the organization. Although unsettling, organized anarchy can be an apt way to understand the organizational structures of institutions of higher education.

It is clear that no one organizational theory explains how colleges and universities are constructed and how decisions are made within those institutions. It is also clear that the informed practitioner should see organizational theory as one of the foundations for practice in student affairs.

Implications for Graduate Preparation Programs

For many years, there has been an internal debate in student affairs regarding the foundations of the profession. Those debates have been useful, but, at times, they have deteriorated into an acceptance of a certain point of view or orthodoxy as the only correct point of view. Graduate preparation programs have been characterized by curricula focused on one of three philosophical and theoretical points of view: counseling, student affairs, and administration. The complexities of the roles that new student affairs professionals must assume in complicated and ever-changing organizations require a new perspective on graduate education for student affairs professionals.

This analysis has confirmed Nuss's point of view (2003), that despite differences, there are two fundamental assumptions that guide the philosophy of student affairs: the development of the whole person and the support of the academic mission of the institution. Belief in those two concepts is not inconsistent with belief in a variety of student development theories, nor is it in conflict with prevailing organizational theories. The crux of the conflict seems to be on the concept of supporting the academic mission of the institution. Support of the academic mission does not mean that student affairs professionals have to be irresponsible and unquestioning—it just means that student affairs professionals need to understand the educational role of the institution and work to support the positive aspects of that role. Graduate education programs should support those principles.

It is also critical that ethics, and an understanding of ethical obligations of professionals in student affairs, should be an essential element in every graduate education program, whatever the particular curriculum emphasis. Too often, ethical behavior has been assumed and is not discussed in graduate education programs.

In addition, all graduate students in preparation programs should understand the two distinct theory strands that inform the work of student affairs. The first theory strand focuses on the development of individual students and their unique characteristics and those of the groups to which they may belong. The second strand focuses on the larger organization that student affairs is a part of in any college or university.

The foundations of student affairs are broad and deep, and graduate preparation programs also need to encourage students to examine both the history of higher education and the history of student affairs. Understanding the foundation of the profession will help graduate students make better choices about institutional and philosophical congruence in their future professional positions.

Finally, there are many roles to fill in student affairs and many ways to fulfill those roles that meet the philosophical, ethical, and theoretical foundations of the student affairs profession. Just as everyone in student affairs does not have to be a vice president, neither do they have to be a counselor or a theoretician. They need, instead, to be active learners in their professional roles and to be very cognizant of their own knowledge and skill limitations in order to be successful.

The graduate faculty in student affairs needs to assume the leadership for broadening the scope and knowledge base of all preparation programs. The profession will be richer for it as will the students and the institutions the profession serves.

Suggestions for Action

The following suggestions are offered for consideration by the profession.

1. *Periodically reinforce the foundations of the profession*. Students change, institutions change, and so do advances in knowledge. The profession, through its professional associations, should periodically review the foundations of the profession and explicitly add additional building blocks as new knowledge and insights become available. In addition, all graduate education programs, regardless of emphasis, should focus on both student development and organizational theories. Failure to provide both theoretical perspectives to graduate students limits the knowledge that they need to work effectively within the larger context of higher education.

2. *Invest time on the foundations of the profession in staff development programs*. Often student affairs supervisors have assumed that there is a shared understanding of the foundations of the profession among their campus and professional colleagues. That is simply not the case. Staff members within a division of student affairs, as discussed elsewhere in this volume, come from a variety of academic and personal experience backgrounds. Discussion of the foundations of the profession helps develop understandings and support among

staff members, whose experiences and knowledge of theories are very diverse.

3. *Place an emphasis on ethics*. Professional associations, student affairs officers, and practitioners all need to place an emphasis on ethics in work and in their interactions with students, faculty, staff, parents, and colleagues. In a world where ethical behavior is sometimes not clear, it is more important than ever for student affairs professionals to be intentional about commitments to ethical behavior.

4. *Support and encourage graduate education programs that prepare student affairs practitioners*. Individual practitioners, as well as professional organizations, should find new and innovative ways to support graduate education programs related to student affairs. Many new professionals come to the field from this arena, and practice cannot be separated from the formal learning environment that such graduate students experience.

Consideration should be given to the creative development of joint degree programs between student affairs preparation programs and other academic programs, such as law, curriculum development, and business. In addition, the curriculum should reflect an emphasis on understanding the differences between and among different institutional types (community colleges, liberal arts institutions, small colleges, regional institutions, and comprehensive universities), with emphasis on the influence that institutional type can have on the development and implementation of student affairs programs and services.

Finally, skilled and knowledgeable practitioners should lend their expertise to graduate programs within their institution and in the surrounding area. Practitioners can help students who are grappling with new theoretical perspectives to translate theory into practice. Such collaborations can occur in formal teaching assignments or by providing support for internships, graduate assistantships, and other work opportunities for graduate students within the student affairs organization.

5. *Stop the arguments and test the theories*. At times, the debates in student affairs have focused on which set of theories or which philosophical statement best demonstrates a *specific point of view*. Assumptions are made, by some, that if persons find organizational theory useful and helpful in their work, they must not understand the value of developmental theory. Or if persons value developmental theory, they cannot understand the broader organizational context of higher education. Each set of theories should be tested and research encouraged on new perspectives in both developmental and organizational theories as they emerge. The theoretical foundations of student affairs focus both on students and on organizations. Both are valuable perspectives to practitioners.

Summary

We are a profession that now has the maturity to support multiple theoretical and professional practice approaches. The work of student affairs has expanded to include work with individual students, student groups, and the management of complex enterprises. Orthodoxy is not the answer! The informed and broadly prepared practitioner will be better equipped to meet the challenges of tomorrow.

In the future, student affairs will continue to grow and evolve. New perspectives and theories will emerge and inform professional practice. The foundation of the profession also will continue to be expanded.

2

Where Should Student Affairs Be Placed Within the Organizational Structure of the Institution?

The range of programs and activities associated with student affairs varies from institution to institution and can include professionals in admissions, orientation, registration, counseling, housing, financial aid, recreational sports, career development, student activities, student health, and many other departments. Student affairs has expanded dramatically during the past forty years and has become a significant part of the administrative organization of most colleges and universities. As a result, it is not surprising that a debate has emerged about where the student affairs division should be placed within the overall organization of the institution. Most often, this debate has focused on one question: "Should the senior student affairs officer report to the president or to the provost?" But this debate goes beyond this one simple question and is a part of a larger issue: "How can student affairs organizations best position themselves to help their institutions achieve their educational missions?"

This chapter opens with a brief review of how student affairs organizations began, and then a discussion of some of the turmoil within the profession that contributed to the debate about organizational structure is presented. New roles for student affairs leaders are discussed, and various models for organizing student affairs are presented. Finally, suggestions for action are offered regarding the organization of student affairs.

A Brief Background

In order to engage effectively in the current debate and to move forward, it is important to understand and learn lessons from our history.

An Important Issue

How student affairs is organized on the campus is an important issue facing the student affairs profession in 2006, as competition for resources becomes more intense, as expectations from students for service increase, as greater public scrutiny is given to what students are actually learning, and as technology continues to change the way education is delivered. The issue is important as well because the effectiveness of the student affairs organization on the campus affects the quality of students' educational experiences. The issue is complicated by the fact that there is still little agreement within the student affairs profession itself about its proper role on the campus.

This debate about how and where to position the student affairs organization is very important to leaders within the profession, because if it is not confronted with vigor and forthrightness, it most likely will be resolved by others outside the profession. If those with little or no knowledge of or commitment to student affairs make decisions about the organizational status of student affairs, the consequences for the profession and for the education of students could be quite serious. It is for this reason that the student affairs organization itself and its placement within the institution has been identified as one of the critical issues needing careful attention within the profession.

The Early Years

It can be argued that when President Charles Eliot appointed a young English instructor, LeBaron Russell Briggs, to be the dean of Harvard College in 1890, this marked the beginning of what is now called student affairs. When student affairs professionals have discussed this appointment over the years, it may have been elevated to a level of importance inconsistent with the way it was viewed at that time. President Eliot, certainly one of the boldest and most innovative leaders in the history of American higher education, was named Harvard president in 1869 and served for forty years in this role. In the twenty-one years before he appointed Briggs to the new position of dean of the College, Eliot struggled mightily in reforming the Medical School, in creating the Graduate School, and in moving and reinvigorating the Law School (Morison, 1936). Of course, during this same time, he also introduced one of the most revolutionary ideas in higher education—the elective system. As a result of these major changes that he had initiated, he faced major opposition from faculty, alumni, and even the Harvard Corporation. In 1885, he knew that "one false step would have meant the end of his administration" (Morison, 1936, p. 359).

When Eliot appointed Briggs to the new position of dean of the College in 1890, he actually "split" the existing dean's position in two: there was now to become an academic dean and a student affairs dean, and when this happened, the "boundaries" for the profession began to develop (Caple, 1998, p. 17). Certainly, the appointment of Briggs was done as much to free the beleaguered president from some of his many obligations as it was to continue the college's commitment to collegiate values. The appointment of the young Briggs was not greeted with much enthusiasm by the faculty, and Briggs was a one-man "organization" with no job description, and only the vaguest of expectations of what he was to do. That he succeeded in becoming one of the most beloved and legendary deans in the profession's history is both an indication of his genius and a lesson for current practitioners. Did his effectiveness depend upon his title, his reporting relationship, or where he was placed on Harvard's organizational chart?

Similar appointments at other institutions followed Briggs's appointment at Harvard in 1890. Among the most notable of these were Alice Freeman Palmer and her associate, Marion Talbot, at the University of Chicago, Lois Kimball Mathews at the University of Wisconsin, Esther Lloyd-Jones at Northwestern University, and Thomas Arkle Clark at the University of Illinois. Colleges were being transformed into universities; faculty were now expected to be scholars and specialists; graduate programs were being established; and the curriculum was expanding rapidly. The new undergraduate deans certainly made life easier for presidents, but they also represented an effort to retain some of the humane values of the old-time colleges. The deans who succeeded in their early work faced many obstacles on the campus. Lois Kimball Mathews, reflecting on her appointment as the first dean of women at Wisconsin, said, "The Dean of Women had her own way to make and her position to form in the midst of all sorts of difficulties. There was real antipathy to the appointment of women on faculties composed almost exclusively of men. Appointed under such circumstances, the new dean had to make good against tremendous odds in which personality and charm weighed out of all proportion to their real importance" (1915, p. 11).

Deans Defining Their Own Roles

Although the first deans were formally responsible to the president, it is clear that most of them essentially created and defined their roles on their own. When Stanley Coulter was appointed dean at Purdue, he inquired of the governing board what his duties might be and was informed that "they did not know but when I found out to let them know!" (Secretarial Notes, 1924, p. 9). The experience of Thomas Arkle Clark at Illinois was similar: "I had no specific duties, no specific authority, no precedents either to guide me or to handicap me. It was an untried sea upon which I was about to set sail. My only chart was the action of the Board of Trustees when they said I was to interest myself in the individual student" (Secretarial Notes, 1924, p. 9).

Eugenie Leonard, in writing about the origins of personnel services in higher education, said, "Presidents could no longer personally supervise the study halls, assign students to rooms, or tramp the dormitory halls at midnight. They did not have the time to buy the food or teach the students table manners. Disciplinary problems had to be delegated, along with control of the numerous student activities to designated personnel in charge of student affairs" (1956, p. 114). Thus the early deans could not rely upon any "inherent powers" of their newly created positions for their effectiveness, or upon a clearly drawn organizational chart that defined their roles. Without the benefit of clear direction from anyone, they were largely on their own and had to establish their own roles.

Student Affairs as a Unique Entity

Frederick Rudolph, commenting on the increasing complexity of universities around the turn of the century, said, "Administrative responsibility was necessarily splintered; first, a secretary of the faculty, then a registrar, and then in succession a vice president, a dean, a dean of women . . . and in time a corps of administrative assistants to the president" (1962, p. 435). Fenske (1989, p. 31) added, "Student services were separated from academics, were professionalized, and became, like business affairs, part of the administration." Thus, even in the earliest years of the profession, student affairs struggled with its identity on the campus: Was it part of the faculty, part of the administration, or did it occupy some ambiguous position between the two? How this issue has been addressed has had a profound impact on the practice of student affairs and where it is placed within the administrative and academic structure of the campus.

Student Affairs as Separate from the Academic Program

Fenske (1989, p. 39) argued that "student affairs has always been separate from the main academic function of teaching and research." Despite vigorous efforts to integrate the curriculum and the extra curriculum, student affairs has often remained separate from the formal educational program of the campus. Indeed, in the most influential document ever published in the field, *The*

Student Personnel Point of View (American Council on Education, 1937), the authors argued that the gap between the student and the formal curriculum was too great.

W. H. Cowley, the most distinguished historian of the field, said of student services, "You do many different kinds of things, but all of them have one distinctive characteristic, namely, they occur outside the formal curriculum" (1964, p. 217). According to Fenske, there has been a "consistent strain of criticism of the profession's status, much of it self-consciously aimed at the low degree of acceptance by faculty and academic administrators" (1989, p. 42). Hopkins (1948) joined this lament, asking "Why should we put ourselves so clearly on the defensive? Why should we show such lack of confidence?" (p. 96). Some years later, Hardee (1961) went even further: "It is obvious that some personnel workers have been so much concerned with problems tangential to the major concerns of higher education that they have operated on the periphery, circling aimlessly in outer space, with resulting ineffectiveness for the main business of the campus, which is learning" (p. 124). This criticism seemed to reach an apex when Penny (1969) stated that "student personnel workers tend to be relegated to subordinate and peripheral positions as middle and lower level administrators . . . because the profession's functions are viewed as mere housekeeping by others in the academic community" (p. 961).

The Dean of Men and the Dean of Women

For a period of almost sixty years, the dean of men and the dean of women defined the primary organization for student affairs functions on the campus. These deans were most often responsible directly to the president and at many institutions exerted a very positive influence on student life. Their roles accurately reflected the differing societal expectations for women and men during the years 1910 through 1965. The professional associations formed to represent their interests and assist in their continuing development spent much of their time discussing the appropriate role for the dean and pleading for more acceptance in the academic community. Whether it was because of a lack of self-confidence or uneasiness about not being in a position of power, many in student affairs continued to be uncomfortable with their place in the administrative and academic structure of the institution. This dilemma undoubtedly stimulated much of the debate about what the most important role of student affairs should be. Moreover, the obvious duplication of duties and sometimes strained relationships between deans of men and deans of women certainly contributed to increased confusion about how best to organize student affairs and skepticism on the part of faculty and academic administrators about its role.

Turmoil Within the Profession

In the years that followed, the role of student affairs was not yet clearly defined. This was a period of ambiguity and no clear direction.

Fragmentation

Contributing further to the problems caused by the ambiguity about the role student affairs role on the campus was the fact that "as a professional field, student affairs has suffered from a fragmentation and proliferation of organizations, which stems in part from its inability to define itself in concrete and specific terms or to agree on a common definition of student personnel work" (Bloland, 1972, p. 102). Among the many professional associations in student affairs, Fenske notes that a consensus about purpose has never been reached within the profession, and "the frequent encounters, withdrawals, rapprochements, and disengagements have resembled the proverbial mating dance of the porcupine" (p. 44). His biting criticism of the field continued with this indictment: "If the medical profession can be characterized as a mighty oak with a massive trunk supporting sturdy branches, the student services profession resembles a disorderly thicket of stunted saplings, each fighting the others for its place in the sun and the crowded, tangled roots all seeking sustenance from the same inadequate source" (Fenske, 1989, p. 27). Finally, the historians Brubacher and Rudy (1976,

p. 346) point out that "many educators have remained profoundly suspicious of the personnel movement, and . . . have reserved their greatest wrath for those institutions which sponsored the organization of an independent personnel division . . . but not as part of the regular instructional faculty." If one can acknowledge only some partial truth in these observations, it is not surprising that there has been so much confusion about the role of student affairs and its proper place within the administrative structure of the institution!

Expansion and Attempts at Definition

After the Second World War, the student affairs field expanded significantly, reflecting the huge increases in enrollment and the rising expectations of students for service. There was a need to coordinate and organize the various services into one organization, and the position of the senior student affairs officer was established for this purpose (Sandeen, 1991). During this same period, several new efforts were made to redefine the field and give it the direction it had presumably lacked in the past. Key among the major goals of these efforts was to make student affairs a viable partner in the academic program of the institution. Brown (1972), Chickering and Reisser, (1993), Kuh, Schuh, and Whitt (1991), Banning and Strange (2001), and Hurst, Morrill, and Oetting (1980) were among the leading writers who advocated student development, campus ecology, educational outcomes, and other approaches as the needed focus for student affairs. At the same time, others described an administrator role (Ambler, 1989), a counselor role (Forrest, 1989), or some combination of a rational, bureaucratic, collegial, or political role (Ambler, 2000).

Despite all the turmoil within the profession, the lack of a clear direction or purpose, the ambiguity of working between the faculty and the administration, and, especially, being considered by many as apart from the core educational program of the institution, student affairs continued to grow and even to prosper during the years after 1965. New demands were placed upon student affairs professionals, many new services and programs were established, and student affairs divisions became large and complex organizations on the campuses. Many senior student affairs officers proved their effectiveness as campus leaders, managers, and mediators and as a result helped student affairs become a vital part of the administrative and management teams of their institutions.

Stature of the Profession Grows

Student affairs professionals faced the most daunting challenges in the profession's history during the years of societal unrest that encompassed the civil rights movement and the Vietnam War. The campuses became one of the primary stages where the political, social, and moral issues of the times were acted out, and student affairs leaders were severely tested. In the process, many of them achieved a level of visibility on the campus and in their communities that far exceeded what they had previously known. At many colleges and universities, student affairs leaders proved themselves to be effective in resolving conflicts, dealing with racial disputes, and keeping the peace. This ability on the part of outstanding deans to handle very difficult problems did more to elevate and advance student affairs on the campus than anything else in the history of the profession. Many faculty, academic administrators, presidents, and board members showed new respect (and in some cases, even admiration) for what student affairs had contributed to the campus. This new recognition enabled some senior student affairs officers to enlarge their divisions, assume responsibility for additional functions, and most important, become a part of the management team of their institutions. The irony of achieving this newfound influence was not lost on many student affairs leaders who had survived those challenges, as they wryly noted that it almost took a student revolution to convince faculty and presidents that they were competent leaders!

Changing Relationship of Students to the Institution

With the revolution in social norms and values of the late 1950s and the early 1960s, the relationship of students to the university underwent significant change. This was especially true for women students,

[handwritten margin note: Deans of men & women phased out]

who began to achieve full access to curricular options previously closed to them and to enjoy greater social freedoms on the campus. Student affairs organizations had for many years included deans of men and deans of women, reflecting the traditional gender-based views and social expectations of society. With the rapid changes taking place in the country, it was not surprising that most colleges and universities reorganized their student affairs divisions along functional lines, and the long-standing titles of dean of men and dean of women began to be phased out, being replaced by the title dean of students, or vice president for student affairs (Sandeen, 1991).

With the position of senior student affairs officer now established and most often reporting directly to the president, student affairs leaders felt they were in the best position they had ever been to contribute to the educational program of the institution. They were colleagues with the senior academic, financial, and development officers, and by demonstrating their ability to manage several major departments on their campuses, they affirmed their value to their institutions.

Shift in Leadership Skills in Student Affairs

During this same time, it became increasingly evident that conflict resolution and crisis management skills—which student affairs leaders had demonstrated so effectively in the past—were often now superseded by the needs of institutions for enrollment management, academic support services, health education, and personal counseling. Some student affairs professionals, who had earned respect for their ability to handle major campus conflicts, found the transition to their new roles as service providers difficult. Moreover, student affairs had now developed an impressive and growing research-oriented literature of its own, and writers such as Brown (1972), Chickering and Gamson (1991), Astin (1993), Barr and Upcraft (1990), Kuh (2003), Pascarella and Terenzini (1991, 2005), Love and Estanek (2004), and Kuh, Kinzie, Schuh, and Whitt (2005) demonstrated how student affairs professionals could become effective educational partners in their colleges and universities. A number of insightful statements about the educational role of student affairs were issued by the professional associations (for example, Schroeder, 1996; Blimling and Whitt, 1999; National Association of Student Personnel Administrators and others, 1998), and these provided additional encouragement to student affairs leaders to become more engaged with the education of students. For the first time in its relatively brief history, student affairs seemed poised to assume a more active and acknowledged role in the educational program of the campus.

New Roles for Student Affairs

In the ensuing years, the profession continued to evolve, as it responded to external events and as it grew internally.

External Influences

Throughout the history of American higher education, events external to the campus, changing demographics, and shifting values have caused colleges and universities to adjust their curricula, their academic policies, and their student services. In 2005, there were over 4,100 colleges and universities in the United States and over fifteen million students. Students reflect the tremendous diversity of the nation and are now bringing to the campus such high expectations for academic and personal support services that many institutions are struggling to find adequate resources to meet what students expect or want. This has placed considerable strains on student affairs divisions, but at the same time, it has often helped them move to a position closer to the core educational programs of their institutions. The seemingly endless needs of students for academic, personal, medical, and psychological support are discussed in more detail in Chapter Six.

Collaboration with Academic Affairs

It was probably inevitable that the changing needs of institutions and the desire of student affairs leaders to become more a part of the educational programs of their campuses would lead to a concerted effort for collaboration with academic affairs (for example, Kellogg, 1999; Banta and Kuh, 1998; Hyman, 1995; Kuh, 1996; Schroeder and Hurst, 1996; Schuh and Whitt, 1999). Developing close and supportive relationships with the senior academic officer, academic deans, and faculty members has become the dominant focus of the profession since 1995. Collaboration became the key word (at least, by student affairs professionals) in describing cooperative efforts in service learning, career services, programs for students with disabilities, student recruitment, orientation, retention, freshman and senior year experience programs, assessment, and other co-curricular programs. On many campuses, this collaboration with academic affairs has succeeded in helping student affairs professionals become more active partners in the educational programs of their institutions. In some cases, it has resulted in the student affairs division moving administratively to academic affairs, with the senior student affairs officer reporting to the provost. While such arrangements were becoming more common, there still was uncertainty about the most effective placement of student affairs within the organizational structure of the institution.

Searching for an Effective Administrative Model

A Centralized Model

After 1965, a centralized, unified student affairs division led by a senior student affairs officer, reporting to the president, became the dominant organizational model (Sandeen, 1991). It had taken student affairs several decades to achieve this organizational status and access to the president that it now enjoyed on most campuses, but with changing institutional needs and student demographics, different organizational arrangements emerged that signaled that this centralized model was by no means permanent, or perhaps still useful. It is not surprising that some student affairs leaders viewed this changing situation with alarm, apprehensive that they might lose their hard-won administrative status on the campus.

Influence of Technology

This situation was further complicated by rapid advancements in technology, enabling students to gain access to services via the Web at any time. Some student affairs divisions became more decentralized, especially on large campuses, with various services, such as financial aid, career services, and academic support services being assumed by academic units. This was especially the case on campuses with extensive professional schools, such as veterinary medicine, law, dentistry, and medicine. At other colleges and universities, the student affairs division itself was no longer directly responsible to the president, but to the provost, or the senior academic affairs officer. At the same time, some student affairs divisions remained centralized, and due to the demonstrated managerial success of the senior student affairs officer, assumed new responsibilities not traditionally considered part of student affairs—such as campus security, personnel, parking and transportation, and intercollegiate athletics.

No Single Model Fits All Institutions

By the year 2000, it was clear that there was no single student affairs organizational model that would fit the needs of all institutions. It also was now clear that a primary goal of student affairs leaders was how to become a vital part of the educational program of their institutions. However, the debate about which administrative model would enable student affairs leaders to achieve this educational goal would continue. In a study of highly successful, senior student affairs officers who had remained in their positions for at least twenty years, the organizational structure for student affairs was found to vary widely from one campus to another (Sandeen, 2001a). Instead of any particular administrative arrangement being related to success, it was found that strong leadership skills, developing positive relationships with constituent groups, and persistence were the factors that successful senior student affairs leaders had in common.

Some Reporting Options

The following models describe reporting options for senior student affairs officers.

Reporting to the President

Reporting directly to the president of the institution may provide the senior student affairs officer easier access to the resource allocation process and may encourage greater understanding of student needs on the part of the president (Barr, 1993; Sandeen, 2001b; Ambler 1993). Equally as important, reporting to the president is likely to place the senior student affairs officer on an equal status with the senior academic, financial, and development officers on the institution's management team. Competition for resources among the senior administrative officers is often intense, and if the senior student affairs officer is not a regular and equal participant in this competition, student affairs programs may not get fair consideration in budgetary decisions.

Being an articulate and persuasive advocate regarding institutional policy is critically important for senior student affairs officers, and reporting directly to the president may provide the best opportunity for this to occur. However, reporting directly to the president carries with it no guarantee that student affairs programs, policies, and needs will be adequately understood, appreciated, or supported. A "stand-alone" student affairs division may appear attractive, but it may reinforce the notion of separation from the rest of the campus, especially from core educational programs. Moreover, if a substantial portion of the budget for student affairs functions is generated by student fees or comes from auxiliary sources, the president and other senior institutional officers may not view student affairs as a direct participant in the campus educational or budgetary program.

Because of the demands of their positions, many college and university presidents now spend most of their time in external activities, such as fundraising, community relations, and legislative-governmental affairs. As a result, reporting directly to the president may, in fact, be illusory for student affairs, as the actual, internal administration of the institution may have been delegated to the provost or to an executive vice president. This situation is becoming much more common, and of course, it complicates the debate about where student affairs should be placed in the administrative structure of the institution. There is often a significant difference between what appears on an official administrative chart of the college or university and what actually happens in the decision-making process. The best student affairs leaders understand this reality.

Reporting to the Provost

Reporting directly to the provost may provide student affairs with the best opportunity it can find to become an actual part of the core educational program of the institution. The provost on most campuses controls most of the institutional budget, has wide-ranging responsibilities, and is directly in charge of academic programs. There may be greater understanding and commitment to student affairs if it is part of the provost's division, and budgetary support may actually improve. It has been true for decades that the provost is "first among equals" within the group of the senior administrators for academic, financial, development, and student affairs. In growing numbers of institutions, the provost has been, in effect, the internal president, and is often more visible on the campus than the president.

When the senior student affairs officer reports to the provost and becomes part of that division, it may become more likely that the various needs, problems, and priorities of student affairs will gain better appreciation and support from academic deans and faculty. With the formal acknowledgment by the institution that there is now a *vice provost for student affairs*, there may be greater acceptance of what student affairs professionals do and an understanding that its activities are an important part of the overall educational program. Perhaps most important, reporting directly to the provost may help discredit the notion that student affairs is a separate entity on the campus. Real collaboration between student affairs professionals and academic deans and faculty might become more frequent and even become second nature if everyone is part of the provost's staff.

Reporting directly to the provost may sentence student affairs to a secondary role on the campus, causing it to lose the visibility and influence it might have enjoyed if it still reported directly to the president. By reporting to the provost, student affairs might be acknowledging certain limits on its overall authority and institutional interests. In its zeal to become part of the *core educational program* by being part of the provost's division, student affairs may be relinquishing some of its possible impact, especially in institution-wide concerns not directly related to student affairs. When student affairs reports directly to the president and is part of the institutional management team with the senior officers for academic, financial, and development affairs, the senior student affairs officer may have more independence and potential impact than if he or she reports to the provost.

A strong senior student affairs officer will occasionally disagree with the other senior administrative officers on the campus on the allocation of resources, the construction or location of new facilities, the establishment of a new policy, or the termination of a program; if the senior student affairs officer is a part of the provost's staff, there may not be a direct and regular forum in which to do this. Of course, reporting to the provost does not ensure that student affairs programs will gain greater visibility among the faculty— or even bring student affairs closer to the core educational program of the institution. Most provosts now have wide-ranging administrative portfolios, and the senior student affairs officer who reports to the provost may be just one of several administrators in that large division. Rather than representing a true commitment to bring academic and student affairs together, this arrangement may actually represent little more than a convenient way to assign reporting roles on the campus. Thus, merely moving the student affairs division to the provost's office does not ensure effective collaboration between student affairs and academic functions, increased funding, or improved understanding and support for what student affairs professionals do.

Decentralized Approach

Decentralizing various student affairs functions into major academic units on the campus is another organizational option. At large universities with several colleges and professional schools, such programs as admissions, orientation, financial aid, service learning, career services, and academic advising may be the direct responsibility of these academic units. In some cases, some of the responsibility for these functions may be shared with the central student affairs organization. When student affairs professionals are clearly identified with a particular academic unit on the campus (such as the College of Engineering), it may be more likely that their interests and expertise might be reflected in the educational program of that academic unit. They might have more frequent and personable relationships with the faculty and engage in joint programs of benefit to students. But of course, even with such a decentralized model, it is very possible that student affairs staff may be viewed as merely service providers, separate from the core educational activities of the academic unit. Reporting to an academic dean and being part of the ongoing discussions in that unit may appear on paper to be the ideal administrative arrangement for effective collaboration between student affairs and academic affairs, but it certainly is no guarantee that this will occur.

Decentralized-Centralized Approach

On some large and complex campuses, some functions may be provided on a centralized basis, whereas others are decentralized to various colleges or divisional units. For example, admissions, financial aid, and health services might be campus-wide, centralized functions, and academic advising, judicial affairs, and career services might be decentralized into the various major academic units. Coordination and consistency can become important challenges in this option, especially if some settings are perceived as more attractive work environments than others, if financial compensation for staff may differ, or if policies may vary. But this model also can provide good opportunities for collaboration, especially with faculty and academic leaders. For those who insist upon a single, clear mission and identity for the student affairs division itself, this model may not be very attractive.

Suggestions for Action

It is not being argued here that the placement of the student affairs division within the organizational structure of the campus is unimportant. Student affairs leaders should give careful attention to the administrative arrangement for their divisions and should analyze the advantages and disadvantages of various options. But as indicated earlier in this chapter, there is no solid evidence that administrative structure alone makes any substantial difference in the overall success of the student affairs program. The following suggestions are made to student affairs leaders regarding organizational structure.

1. *Student affairs leaders should focus on gaining access to institutional resources.* Their position location on the campus organizational chart is far less important in achieving resources than is their ability to articulate the needs of their division in a clear and persuasive manner. Student affairs leaders should "follow the money" on their campuses and demonstrate by their actions what the real benefits of their programs and policies are to their institutions.

Through their positive contributions, knowledge, and insight, student affairs leaders should make themselves indispensable participants in the institutional decision-making process. Reporting directly to the president does not ensure this will happen; student affairs leaders must earn their place at the decision-making table, regardless of the formal organizational arrangement at their institutions. This will require them to be very well informed, able to make data-based contributions to the budgetary and decision-making process.

2. *Student affairs leaders must be strongly committed to student learning as the primary focus for their work.* Regardless of the organizational or administrative structure at their institutions, it is their responsibility to initiate and build collaborative programs with the provost, academic deans, and department chairs, and with the faculty. Student affairs leaders do not have to report to the president for this to happen; it is a matter of leadership, and if student affairs leaders do not take the initiative, it is unlikely that others on campus will do so.

3. *Student affairs leaders should understand that their role is to persuade, to advocate, and to produce successful results for their students and for their institutions.* They rarely achieve anything significant on their campuses in isolation from others. If they think a lofty title or position on the campus organizational chart will convince others of the benefits of changed policies or new programs, they are fooling themselves. Leadership in student affairs demands taking chances—with ideas, programs, and policies. The best student affairs professionals know how to present, defend, and implement their ideas.

4. *Student affairs leaders should educate themselves about the most important issues at their institutions, regardless of where their positions may be located on the campus organizational chart.* They are expected to be highly knowledgeable about student affairs issues, of course. But they should also be able to make important contributions to the academic, research, and development programs at their institutions. They should be visible, frequent participants in all aspects of their institutions. It is their competence, knowledge of higher education issues, courage, and personal integrity that will earn them a significant role on the campus, not their place on the organizational chart.

Summary

Student affairs as a formal entity has only been part of higher education for about a hundred years. During this time, it has evolved into a vital component of virtually all colleges and universities. Significant changes have taken place in how student affairs is organized and where it is placed in the structure of the institution. The various models for the organization of student affairs will continue to be debated, and this is a healthy activity for the profession. However, the most important issue for student affairs is not where it is placed on the organizational chart, but how effective its leadership is on the campus.

3

How Should Student Affairs Help Students Learn About Diversity?

D iversity has probably received more attention than any other issue in American higher education during the past forty years.

A Brief Background

American colleges and universities have served as a primary stage for the testing of major social issues during the past forty years.

An Awakening Social Conscience

When the American social conscience was awakened by the civil rights movement, the country began to get serious about its efforts to remove barriers that limited access and opportunity to millions of its citizens for many generations. The early focus was primarily on securing increased access and rights for African Americans and women, but it expanded to include other racial minorities, religion, persons with disabilities, age, and sexual orientation. Discussion about these issues often was volatile and became a prominent part of political debates, even in presidential elections. Affirmative action became a highly public issue, resulting in Supreme Court decisions (Pope, Reynolds, and Mueller, 1978; Gratz, 2003; Grutter, 2003) that reflected the divisions still evident in the country. State and federal laws were often passed to ensure that the rights of all citizens were protected. But most Americans understood that if the ideals of a democratic society were to be realized, simply removing barriers and enacting new laws would not be sufficient. The most important goals were tolerance, understanding, appreciation of differences, and inclusion. These would become the real challenges of diversity.

College as Gateway to Success

As colleges and universities serve as almost the exclusive gateway to economic, professional, and social advancement in American society, it was natural that they quickly became a primary focus for efforts to remove barriers and improve access. Even though the initial efforts to improve access and remove barriers were often difficult, significant gains were achieved over the years, as colleges and universities across the country admitted and graduated students from much broader backgrounds than ever before. But academic leaders understood that their role extended far beyond removing barriers and improving access. They knew their most important goal as educators was to help students learn to be effective citizens and leaders in a complex society, where differences in race, religion, ethnicity, sexual orientation, physical ability, and gender could be understood and celebrated. They embraced diversity in their institutional missions, in their teaching, and in the educational content and objectives of their academic departments. In many cases, institutions developed academic courses that addressed the goals of diversity and added requirements to their general education programs that introduced students to non-Western ideas, multiculturalism, and other topics related to diversity. In an effort to make their institutions more effective settings for learning, colleges and universities recruited faculty and students who more closely reflected the tremendous diversity of the country and the world.

Student Life a Focus of Diversity

It was in student life where diversity issues became most visible and sometimes volatile. With large numbers of students from previously underrepresented or unacknowledged populations—women, racial and ethnic minorities, persons with disabilities, and gay, lesbian, bisexual, and transgender students—the campus became a testing ground for democratic ideals and values that were frequently espoused by the larger society but not often practiced by it. With most students growing up in relatively homogeneous communities, what would happen when these same students encountered peers from backgrounds and personal orientations very different from their own? Most student interaction, of course, took place in student residences, fraternities and sororities, recreational sports, campus dining halls, and student organizations. Many college leaders were anxious about the ability of their institutions to accommodate the new students. Responding to the tumultuous social changes in American society in the mid-1960s, colleges and universities recruited previously underrepresented students in significant numbers but often did not plan effectively in providing the necessary academic, social, and financial support for these students. As a result, many of these students felt exploited, isolated, or embittered (Hossler and Bean, 1990; Feagin, 1996).

Challenges to Student Affairs

This time of great societal change presented student affairs with the most daunting challenges in its history. Student affairs leaders were expected to be peacemakers, conflict resolvers, mediators, and community builders. In a climate often characterized by political distrust, social unrest, and racial misunderstanding, student affairs leaders were expected to help their institutions retain their civility, decrease their bureaucracy, and above all, build humane and trusting relationships with students, many of whom felt alienated from their campuses. The college campus became the primary stage where American society would put its most volatile ideas on trial—access, tolerance, political dissent, and cultural pluralism—and student affairs professionals were front and center. Some flourished in this climate, serving their institutions and their students with outstanding leadership; others found that their talents, energy, or backgrounds were not sufficient to meet the new challenges and left the profession.

Expanding Literature and Research

The literature of American higher education during this period is voluminous; for example, the dozens of volumes in the Carnegie Council on Policy Studies in Higher Education (1980) series were published as a direct result of the rapid social changes taking place in society. A great deal of the writing and research was addressed to diversity issues (for example, Hsia and Hirono-Nakanishi, 1989; McCune, 2001; McEwen, 2002; Sanlo, Rankin, and Schoenberg, 2002; Schmidt, 2003; Torres, 2003; Tierney, 1991; Wall and Evans, 1999). From 1965 to the present time, considerable progress was made by colleges and universities in improving access, removing barriers, making campuses more inclusive, improving racial and ethnic understanding, and encouraging civility. This is quite remarkable, given the "fraying of America" (Hughes, 1992) and the almost four decades of raucous and bitter struggles over affirmative action, hate speech codes, court decisions, ethnic studies, admissions standards, separate cultural houses, "political correctness," faculty-hiring practices, violence against women and minorities, state legislation, and many other issues. But a great deal more remains to be done, as colleges and universities still have much to learn about how to make their campuses humane, inclusive, and supportive settings for student learning.

Student Affairs and Diversity

As times changed, student affairs had to change too.

The History of Student Affairs Reflects
Dominant Societal Values

It might be reassuring to current student affairs leaders to believe that a strong commitment to diversity has been a core belief and practice in the field from its beginning. However, there is very little evidence to support such an assertion. Some of the early deans (for example, Talbot, 1910) were champions of the underrepresented (especially women) on their campuses and advocated greater rights for students, but for the most part, the undergraduate curriculum and student life quite clearly reflected the dominant values of the larger society. Discrimination in admissions on the basis of race, religion, and gender continued to be practiced by many colleges and universities for several decades, including through the 1950s (Levine, 1986; Freedman, 2000), and general education programs for undergraduate students focused mainly on Western civilization (Gaff and Ratcliff, 1996).

Student life, until the early 1960s, continued to reflect the sex role stereotyping of the larger society, and women and men were subject to different social rules and regulations and even separate student governing groups on most campuses. Women were restricted, either by tradition or by actual policy, from entering certain academic programs, especially in the professions. Students of color and students with disabilities enrolled in very small numbers on predominately *white* campuses (a term not used at the time), and their special needs were not often known or addressed in any concerted way. Students whose sexual orientation was not traditional were virtually invisible on the campus, as homophobic attitudes and downright hostility frequently made their lives miserable (Sanlo, 1999).

The Student Personnel Point of View, 1937

The Student Personnel Point of View (American Council on Education, 1937), which served as the guiding philosophy of the field for decades, was silent on the issue of *diversity* (which, of course, was a word not often in use in 1937). It urged institutions to consider the student as a whole, including his or her moral and religious values, but the main emphasis in the document is upon what student affairs staff can do to help students adjust to the demands of the college. The authors of this highly influential document apparently were not ready to advocate a more active role for colleges and universities or for student affairs in breaking down barriers, improving access, or

educating students about diversity. Deans of women were outspoken advocates for greater access and rights for women students, but
for the most part, student affairs practices during this time accurately reflected the dominant values of society.

World War II and the GI Bill

After the tremendous social upheaval caused by World War II,
colleges and universities expanded in ways unimagined by higher
education leaders, and access provided by the GI Bill brought huge
numbers of previously underrepresented students to the campuses.
Shortly after the war, a revision of *The Student Personnel Point of
View* (American Council on Education, 1949) was published, and
the authors now advocated a much more active role for student
affairs professionals in such areas as international understanding and
cooperation, the application of creative imagination to the solution
of social problems, and the development of students interacting in
social situations. The student affairs literature, the program content
of national conferences, and student life on the campuses after
World War II began to reflect some of the emphasis suggested by
the authors of the 1949 statement, although the McCarthy Era, the
Korean War, and the conservative culture of the 1950s caused student affairs work during that decade to remain quite traditional.

The Civil Rights Movement

It was the national civil rights movement, of course, that caused the
public finally to acknowledge the huge gap that existed between
rhetoric and reality in American life and to think seriously about the
promise of democracy. Many student affairs leaders strongly identified with this movement, finding its goals of equality, access, and fairness very compatible with their own values. Because of the trust they
developed with students, faculty, and community members over the
years, some student affairs deans were able to help their institutions
avoid some of the violence that erupted when racial integration
came to southern campuses (for example, Trillin, 1964). Others were

closely involved in their institution's efforts to recruit minority students and to help them become accepted on the campus. The revolution in women's rights in American society coincided with the civil rights movement, and student affairs organizations, activities, and policies adapted to this change. The emphasis upon treating all students as if they were, in fact, adult citizens was recognized with the publication of one of the most important documents in student affairs history, *The Joint Statement on Rights and Freedoms of Students* (American Association of University Professors and others, 1967).

Student Affairs Leaders Embrace Diversity

Student affairs leaders were engaged in a wide variety of efforts related to diversity. New campus organizational structures were created to address diversity issues; new professional staff were hired whose background seemed especially suited to work with targeted students; cultural and ethnic-based facilities were constructed; new financial resources were secured for academic and student support; special counseling and career services were established; mediation was often conducted with student and community groups; and professional organizations became very active in advocating diversity. Most important within the student affairs community was the recognition and commitment to diversity as an extremely important educational goal. The intensity of the conversation about diversity in American society can hardly be overstated, and within student affairs, it often had a strong moral tone (Bonham, 1983; Young, 1997).

Role of National Legislation

As has always been the case, events in the greater society continued to drive what happened on the campuses. After years of debate and lobbying, the U.S. Congress enacted Section 503 of the Rehabilitation Act in 1973 and the Americans with Disabilities Act in 1991, requiring colleges and universities to ensure equal access and reasonable accommodations for students with disabilities. This legislation made it possible for student affairs staff to acquire the resources and commitments to assist large numbers of students whose needs may have been overlooked earlier or who had previously not been encouraged to enroll. The gay liberation movement in American society faced tremendous obstacles in its efforts to obtain dignity, respect, and acceptance for persons whose sexual orientation was not traditionally heterosexual. The emergence of AIDS as a disease affecting millions of people around the world made the conversation about sexual orientation and acceptance of differences more humane and change more possible. When Mathew Shepard, a young student at the University of Wyoming, died as a result of a homophobic murder (Hurst, 1999), the nation's social conscience was raised again, and the efforts of student affairs staff to help campuses become more accepting, inclusive, and supportive of students of different sexual orientations became more possible.

The best student affairs leaders understood that their role in campus diversity was critical and, especially, that their efforts needed to reach far beyond mere policy change, physical facilities, resource procurement, and organizational adjustments (Sandeen, 2001a). They understood that their most important role was education. Many of them had played important roles in increasing the "mix" of their student bodies in terms of race, gender, ethnicity, religion, disability, and sexual orientation, and most were pleased with the increased heterogeneity of their campuses. But the best student affairs staff knew that simply having students from broader backgrounds did not automatically result in increased understanding, greater tolerance, knowledge of other cultures, or appreciation of differences. They knew that their most important work in the area of diversity was just beginning!

Diversity Becomes a Priority in Student Affairs

The past twenty years in student affairs have been characterized by vigorous and creative efforts to address diversity (for example, Adelman, 1997; Caple, 1990; Chang, 2001; Cortes, 2000; Stewart and Peal, 2001; Wilson, 1996; Vander Putten, 2001). Though there have been many disagreements about what diversity should mean, most would agree that the major goal of diversity education is to produce graduates who will become effective citizens and leaders in a multicultural society. Colleges and universities certainly are not meeting their educational obligations in 2006 if their students are not living, working, and studying in highly diverse campus cultures. The future clearly belongs to those who will be best able to work effectively with people from many backgrounds, orientations, lifestyles, and ways of learning and knowing. In the past twenty years in particular, student affairs staff have not only embraced this goal of diversity education but some of them have adopted it as the core component of their campus programs (Sandeen, 2001b). Yet, additional student needs require attention.

Current Student Affairs Diversity Initiatives

Identifying Unmet or Ignored Student Needs

Most student affairs leaders have been active participants in efforts to make their campuses more accessible, open, accepting, and inclusive. Because of their daily engagement with students, they are aware of the many communities represented on their campuses and the different ways these communities relate to the institution. Their knowledge and insight about student experiences, backgrounds, aspirations, and frustrations have often resulted in better policies, programs, and services. Identifying a previously ignored or unmet need of a group of students on the campus and then helping this group become an appreciated member of the campus community has been among the most important contributions that student affairs leaders have made to their institutions. For example, the "official" government-inspired classification of minorities often masks critical differences within these classifications. The students in the Filipino Association may have connections to Asian American and Hispanic American groups, but as for their own identity and cultural activities, they are unique. Good student affairs staff recognize this and understand that if they are going to help Filipino students become a viable part of campus life, these students will need special attention. They also understand that knowledge of a special culture is essential before any efforts aimed at inclusiveness can be successful.

Professional Development Programs and Diversity

The student affairs profession has been aggressive in providing educational programs about diversity for its members. Diversity has been a major focus for state, regional, and national conferences for many years, and various institutes and seminars have been conducted specifically for the purpose of increasing knowledge about diversity (National Association of Student Personnel Administrators, 2004). The graduate preparation programs in the field have adopted education about diversity and *multicultural competence* in working with students as core goals (Flowers and Howard-Hamilton, 2002; Evans and Phelps Tobin, 1998; Council for the Advancement of Standards in Higher Education, 2003). The professional journals in student affairs and numerous monographs and books have addressed this topic (for example, Whitt and others, 2001; Wright and Tierney, 1991; Pascarella and others, 1996; Rosenblum and Travis, 2000). It is very encouraging to see the advances in student affairs and related literature and research in this area, as important new understandings of how identity is developed within various cultures, how students from various backgrounds learn, and how students perceive their campus environments are explored.

Hiring a Diverse Student Affairs Staff

Student affairs campus organizations were among the first to hire professional staff from previously underrepresented groups. This began rather quietly in the late 1960s before institutions were strongly encouraged by formal affirmative action programs to take such actions. Most senior student affairs officers who initiated such hiring did so because they understood that the important demographic changes taking place among students made this a necessity. With large numbers of new students who were different from those the institution had previous admitted, staff were needed who could relate to their special cultural, financial, social, and academic concerns. Since that early period, the best student affairs organizations have worked hard to ensure that their professional staff includes persons whose ethnic, racial, gender, age, and sexual orientation backgrounds are at least as diverse as that of their students.

Collaboration with Academic Affairs

The current educational efforts by student affairs staff directed at diversity are encouraging and impressive. A large number of colleges and universities have revised their mission statements to reflect their commitment to diversity in all of their programs and have added diversity to their general education requirements. This is also the case in many academic disciplines, where the students seek their educational concentrations. Although some of this change has been slow and only piecemeal in nature, it has provided student affairs staff with an ideal opportunity to collaborate closely with academic affairs leaders and faculty. Dozens of campuses have established first-year learning courses (Gardner and Upcraft, 1989), and because diversity education is a core component of such courses and experiences, all new students can learn more about different cultures, languages, age differences, sexual orientations, racial and ethnic histories, and gender differences. Some campuses also have reintroduced a form of the old *senior seminar,* by focusing on culminating or capstone courses during the final undergraduate year. This focus on the senior year experience (Gardner and Van der Veer, 1998) provides an excellent opportunity for institutions to assess the learning of their graduating students in the area of diversity. On most campuses, student affairs staff have often been the initiators of such courses or have played a significant role in their development and implementation.

Student affairs staff, often in conjunction with faculty colleagues, regularly plan and conduct programs specifically directed at improving the knowledge of differences in culture, race, ethnicity, disability, gender, or sexual orientation. Taking advantage of the knowledge they have gained about their students, both by observation and research, they have invited students to weekend retreats, cultural conferences, and educational seminars that engage the participants in discussions, debates, and exercises designed to challenge their values and assumptions. These student experiences, though often intense and personal, are often identified by the student participants as among the most worthwhile educational experiences they have had in college. Many of the students who have been part of these diversity education experiences become peer educators on the campus, working closely with faculty and student affairs staff to make the campus more inclusive. When presidents, provosts, and academic deans have been participants in such special retreats and seminars, the commitment to diversity and inclusiveness on the campus can take on new meaning for the students.

New Inquiries and Learning About Diversity

New inquiries are now being conducted about diversity and different ways of learning, and the knowledge and understanding gained can be of great benefit to student affairs staff in their work with students. Talbot (1999); Sue (2003); Chickering and Reisser (1993); Astin (1993); Coles (1988); Baxter-Magolda (1992); Pope, Reynolds, and Mueller (2004), and McClellan (1996) are among the most notable who have brought valuable insights and strategies regarding diversity education that student affairs staff have used in their practice. Moreover, the writing and research of Takaki (1993), Turner (1996), Bok and Bowen (2002), Smith and Schonfeld (2000), Lark (1998), Shireman (2003), Hurtado (1999), and Kramer and Weiner (1994) have significantly enriched opportunities to learn about different cultures. The National Survey of Student Engagement Project (Kuh, 2003) can provide colleges and universities with excellent data about how their students actually engage with one another and with their faculty, and such information can be a great value in policy, campus life, advising, and teaching programs.

The current emphasis upon assessment in higher education (Banta, 2002) also provides an excellent opportunity for institutions to evaluate their impact on student attitudes, values, and skills gained during the undergraduate years. Pascarella and Terenzini (1991) have summarized a great deal of this research, and it is evident that colleges and universities who deliberately and consistently engage students in diversity education can produce educational outcomes that are very positive.

Value of Recognizing and Celebrating Diversity

Student affairs staff also understand the value of recognizing and celebrating students and student organizations who reflect the diversity of the campus. Most campuses now have special times set aside for such celebrations, and through drama, art, music, dance, food, and dress, new knowledge and understanding are often dramatically displayed and enjoyed. The widespread popularity of community service programs has provided an ideal opportunity for students from diverse backgrounds to work together for common causes (Bradfield and Myers, 1996). Some student affairs staff have found that the best way to "teach about diversity" is to get students from a variety of backgrounds together, working on a project toward a common goal, over a period of time. Recognizing students, faculty, and staff at major events (such as commencement) who have made positive contributions to the improvement of diversity and inclusiveness can reinforce the commitment made by campus leaders to these goals. Student affairs staff have often been the initiators of such valuable efforts on their campuses.

Many Obstacles Remain

Many formidable obstacles still remain, of course, in the country's yearning for social justice, cultural understanding, and the appreciation of differences. College campuses may represent the best opportunity for young people to learn about diversity, especially because so many students grew up in relatively homogeneous communities. Despite the vigorous efforts of faculty and student affairs staff to engage students in diversity, there is discouraging evidence that many students may prefer to avoid the discomforting questions often raised in such discussions. A prominent national survey of college students (Levine and Cureton, 1998) revealed a reluctance of students to engage in conversations about diversity, perhaps suggesting that large numbers of students are pessimistic about the future or simply tired of pursuing the topic.

Efforts to include diversity in the curriculum have sometimes resulted in disjointed and isolated courses that have little real connection to the lives of students or to their main academic pursuits. When the *diversity requirement* in a general education core can be satisfied by freshmen and sophomores selecting any two courses from among over 350 choices, the likelihood that some coherent understanding about culture, and racial, ethnic, gender, disability, and sexual orientation may emerge is very low. The exploitation and stereotyping of various groups for economic and social reasons, especially as seen in advertising, popular music, television and movies, often contributes to an increasing fragmentation of American society. Young students are among the prime consumers of these powerful images, and the messages transmitted may be quite contrary to what faculty and student affairs staff are struggling to teach on their campuses. The attacks on the World Trade Center and the Pentagon in 2001, and the many military actions (such as the war in Iraq) and guerrilla activities since that time, around the world have obviously made diversity education efforts more difficult, but also increasingly important. The need to help students learn more about other cultures has never been more self-evident, especially in regard to religious differences and understanding. Finally, the increasing emphasis on undergraduate education as job preparation and the legislative pressure placed upon public institutions to graduate students more quickly have provided few incentives for students to explore new courses or ideas during their undergraduate programs that do not serve their immediate vocational goals.

Positive Contributions of Student Affairs

Many student affairs leaders deserve credit for the positive contributions they have made to the diversity of their campuses by improving facilities, changing policies, developing programs, hiring staff, increasing access, securing resources, and enriching educational programs. Moreover, in many cases, student affairs staff have served as positive role models for students when they have mediated volatile issues with sensitivity, invited previously ignored groups into campus life, advocated for just causes others did not have the courage to confront, and insisted upon civility and inclusion as core values. From admissions and orientation, residence halls and judicial affairs to counseling and health services and leadership programs and career advising, student affairs staff have used their knowledge and close relationships with students to teach about diversity.

Suggestions for Action

The following suggestions are offered for consideration by the profession.

1. *Student affairs professionals should continue to strive to treat students as individuals.* For over forty years, many student affairs staff have thought about diversity in terms of groups or categories. For too long, students have been defined or described in relation to their race, age, ethnicity, language, sexual orientation, or disability. This categorization of students is often arbitrary and superficial and contradicts one of the core beliefs of the student affairs profession itself—the uniqueness of each individual student. Thinking about students as "categories" and treating them as members of these so-called groups can distort understandings about individuals and, worse, reinforce societal myths about the characteristics of these "groups." Thinking about diversity in this fashion can result in the continuing fracturing of the campus into competing groups and may actually encourage competition for resources or claims of victimization.

Student affairs leaders will benefit by recognizing that the debate about diversity in American society is still evolving and that it can be most effectively addressed by rethinking their assumptions about diversity. It is not about arbitrary and superficial categories—diversity should be about educational efforts to prepare students to work successfully as citizens and leaders in a multicultural society. Students are individuals and should be treated as such. Their group affiliations may have nothing to do with who they really are, regardless of their race, ethnicity, age, disability, or sexual orientation. Treating them as members of groups can distort educational efforts in diversity and may encourage the very categorization and fragmentation that ought to be avoided.

2. *Student affairs professionals should become strong and visible leaders on their campuses and in their communities on diversity issues.* Simply increasing the "mix" of students is insufficient in preparing students to be effective citizens and leaders in a multicultural world. At a time when others may find it tempting to back away from the often volatile and wrenching efforts to confront differences, student affairs professionals should step to the front and lead, not follow. At times, this leadership role may place them and their jobs in jeopardy, when they become outspoken advocates for social justice or inclusion of students in all campus programs. Seriously educating students about diversity is not a detached, purely intellectual exercise; it can be fraught with controversy and may subject its public advocates to unpleasant scrutiny. Student affairs staff, both by their training and the values of their profession, should be the most visible and effective advocates for diversity on their campuses. And they should be willing and able to accept the consequences of their advocacy and actions.

3. *Student affairs leaders should take the lead in collaborating with their colleagues in academic affairs in establishing educational programs that will help students become effective citizens and leaders in a multicultural society.* If done properly, this will require student affairs staff to become more familiar with the actual content of what undergraduates are currently studying in their classes, an activity too long

ignored by student affairs professionals. Collaboration with faculty in developing new courses and academic experiences for students will become much more possible when student affairs staff are clear about what it is they have to contribute to such efforts. There are good models to emulate, but student affairs staff should assume responsibility for acquiring the knowledge and skills necessary to ensure that they are valuable partners in cooperative efforts with faculty.

4. *Student affairs professionals should assume responsibility for their own continuing education about diversity issues.* Student affairs professionals have often relied on their own observations and personal contacts with students to educate themselves about diversity. Such efforts are very important and should continue to be pursued. However, student affairs professionals should recognize the limitations of such learning. Information and insight gained from scheduled focus group discussions, regular assessments of student perceptions of the campus climate, and reading extensively in the massive literature on multiculturalism are essential activities for student affairs leaders. By leaving the campus and traveling to the communities (and countries) where students live, student affairs staff can greatly expand their awareness and sensitivity. The useful research being conducted about identity development in various cultures is an example of how important it is for student affairs staff to continue to educate themselves about diversity.

5. *Student affairs professionals have many campus and community colleagues in their efforts to help students learn about diversity.* There may be a certain smugness or comfort among some student affairs professionals in thinking they alone are "carrying the torch" for diversity issues on their campuses. No group of professionals in colleges and universities has an exclusive corner on the knowledge, skills, and commitment needed to educate students about diversity. Student affairs staff should never permit themselves to engage in self-congratulation by thinking they are the lone oasis of understanding and tolerance on their campuses. Moreover, senior student affairs officers should intervene if they discover staff who may have personal agendas that obscure or violate their professional commitment to diversity education. All student

affairs professionals should engage in diversity education efforts; they are not the exclusive domain of a few experts.

6. *Student affairs professionals should recognize that they need the support and participation of many others outside student affairs to accomplish their goals in diversity education.* The total student affairs staff on most campuses is very small in relation to the number of faculty. Although it may be easier to develop diversity education programs exclusively conducted by student affairs staff, this isolation will virtually ensure that these efforts will not be a significant part of the overall campus effort in diversity education. Even though collaboration with faculty, student groups, and community organizations is often complicated and slow, it is essential for real success. Student affairs professionals are most often the initiators of such collaborations, and this leadership role is the most critical of all for student affairs staff to assume.

7. *Student affairs leaders should insist that helping students learn about diversity remains a core value of the profession.* It represents the fundamental beliefs of student affairs: tolerance, openness, acceptance, and respect for others. It provides student affairs leaders with perhaps their most important and challenging opportunity to influence the lives of students. Student affairs professionals should be ideally suited to this challenge.

Summary

Helping and encouraging students to learn about diversity is a critically important priority for student affairs. Professionals in this field are ideally suited by their educational backgrounds and commitments to provide leadership to their institutions in improving diversity. Student affairs leaders can be proud of their many efforts in diversity during the past forty years, but many important challenges remain. Opportunities abound for student affairs professionals to collaborate with faculty in making the student experience in higher education truly diverse.

4

How Can Student Affairs Attract
and Retain a Diverse Staff?

The work of student affairs is labor-intensive. Providing help, support, and learning opportunities for individual students and student groups requires professionals willing to interact with students in a variety of settings. It is human work and requires professional staff members who understand both organizational and human development theory and can translate that theory into practices that enhance the educational experience and learning of students. Student affairs work can be life changing, life affirming, frustrating, and difficult, and it can be all of those things all at the same time.

The effectiveness of any student affairs organization is directly linked to the skills, competencies, knowledge, and personal qualities of the staff members who plan, organize, and develop programs and services for students. High-quality professional staff members are key to the success of the enterprise. Therefore, it is important that the student affairs profession focus on hiring and retaining staff that can work effectively with the diverse student populations that make up the enrollment of higher education institutions today. Wilkinson and Rund (2000) indicate, however, that "higher education while at the forefront of educating the larger society about diversity, still falls short of employing a staff that reflects the nation's diversity" (p. 586).

In addition to reflecting the diversity of enrolled students, student affairs staff members also have responsibility to help students who have had little contact with persons who are different from them learn to appreciate and celebrate differences. For the reality of the demographics of this nation is that the current students will sometime in their life be supervised by, work as colleagues with, supervise someone, or live next door to someone who is very different from them in some important way. Students benefit from working with staff members from many backgrounds because they learn about differences on a daily basis and glimpse the workforce they will one day join (Freeman, Nuss, and Barr, 1993). It is clear that if colleges and universities do not effectively aid students in dealing with differences in positive ways, then the future society will suffer.

This chapter will first discuss the rationale for a more diverse staff and will then identify the barriers in attracting and retaining diverse individuals in student affairs. Next, the chapter will identify the challenges inherent in attracting and maintaining a diverse staff in an increasingly competitive environment. Finally, recommendations to be considered by future student affairs officers regarding staffing will be presented.

Importance of Staff Diversity

The issue of staff diversity in higher education has different dimensions than are faced by many other organizations. Brogue (2002) said it best, stating in part that "colleges and universities exist for purposes beyond developing knowledge and skill in our students. They are also sanctuaries of our personal and civic values, and incubators of intellect and integrity. And so the values that mark the community of higher learning are the values that are most likely to be caught by our students" (p. 8).

If, indeed, the purposes of higher education extend beyond knowledge and skills, then each college or university must define what values the institution wants to impart to students.

Institutional values are expressed in many ways within the institution, including resource allocation, the curriculum, the physical setting, artifacts and artworks, the library, the research enterprise, the public statements of institutional leadership, and the demographic characteristics of faculty and staff. For example, if intercollegiate athletics competition is a value embraced by the institution, then competition venues will be built, coaches and athletic staff hired, schedules negotiated, and student athletes recruited. If, on the other hand, the institution values recreational sports rather than intercollegiate competition, then resources will be focused on teaching students lifelong personal health and fitness skills and competencies in order to engage through a range of programs and activities sponsored by the institution.

Diversity is but one of many values embraced by institutions of higher education, and the value of diversity is frequently reflected in public pronouncements and publications by colleges and universities. In addition, the student affairs profession has affirmed the value of diversity many times and in many ways. A *Perspective on Student Affairs* (1989), for example, makes the case for diversity in American colleges and universities stating in part that "it is imperative that students learn to recognize, understand and celebrate human differences. Colleges can, and indeed, must help their students become open to the differences that surround them: race, religion, age, gender, culture, physical ability, language, nationality, sexual preference and lifestyle. These matters are learned best in collegiate settings that are rich in diversity, and they must be learned if the ideals of human worth and dignity are to be advanced" (National Association of Student Personnel Administrators, 1989, p. 12). In addition, the 2003 *Council on the Advancement of Standards: General Standards and Guidelines* places special emphasis on the importance of diversity on college campuses, stating in part that "diversity enriches the collegiate experience for all; therefore programs and services must nurture environments where commonalities and differences among people are recognized and honored" (Council for the Advancement of Standards in Higher Education, 2003, p. 13).

The questions are clear: How can student affairs professionals help students learn about diversity if the staff itself is not diverse? How can student affairs help students learn about differences if there is not a broad range of role models available to interact with students in their daily lives? How may students learn about diversity if their institutional experience is devoid of interactions with faculty and staff who are either like them or different from them in some important way? Komives (1999) indicates that a rich and diverse professional staff enhances the working environment and helps professional staff members continue to grow and develop. Diversity has many dimensions, and when considering how to attract and retain a diverse staff, all of these dimensions must be accounted for in personnel policies and practices.

Barriers

There are a number of barriers to achieving and retaining genuine staff diversity. Each barrier, however, must be assessed, challenged, and multiple strategies developed to overcome the perceived barrier. New ways of attracting and then retaining diverse staff must be found if student affairs is going to be successful in the future. Some of the barriers are discussed in this section.

Unclear Career Path

Brown (1987) said it best when he indicated that students do not grow up with the intention of being student affairs professionals. That notion helps differentiate student affairs from other professions, such as doctor, lawyer, or engineer. At least five pathways are available to someone entering a career in student affairs: intentional decision, unintentional decision, organizational realignment, specialty preparation, and staying through inertia. "When we discuss the profession, however, the intentional-decision individuals provide our model for the ideal student affairs staff member" (Barr,

1990, p. 165). But there are great differences even in academic backgrounds and the personal experiences of individuals who make an intentional decision to enter the field.

Many in student affairs come to the profession unintentionally. A position is open, they meet the minimal qualifications and are hired. They apply for a variety of reasons but do not, at least initially, see student affairs as a long-term commitment to students and the profession. But exposure to the field and to intentional professionals can change ideas, and they can become committed to the field or leave for other opportunities.

Often new staff come to student affairs through organizational changes and realignments. The changing portfolio for student affairs on many campuses is a testament to this phenomenon. Such individuals do not share a common background or understanding of students, programs, and services. Organizationally realigned individuals have the potential to make great contributions to students, student affairs colleagues, and the institution. They may not, however, share a common base of understanding of the assumptions, beliefs, and theories that undergird the work of student affairs.

As indicated earlier, a large number of staff come to student affairs through specialty areas in student affairs and do not see themselves as student affairs professionals at all. They have deep roots in their professional identity and specialty area, such as physician, nurse, psychologist, or coach. Finally, there are those individuals who see student affairs as a means rather than an end—a way to get their foot into the door of higher education without a commitment to the field at all. Why is this important?

Perhaps more than any other staff of the academy, student affairs professional staff reflect the most diversity in training, background, and experiences. Academic departments have clearly defined career credentials and standards for promotion that must be met. Other parts of the institution require specialty training in accounting, business, technology, or the like. The field of student affairs often seems more amorphous and more confusing to the uninitiated. There is not a clear career path to student affairs, and that may make it less attractive to diverse individuals.

Perception of Advancement

Just as there is not a clear career path for entering the profession, there is not a clear career path for advancing within the profession or within the institution. Opportunities for advancement become more restricted the further a person advances up the organizational chart in student affairs. Richmond and Sherman (1991) and Evans (1988) indicate that there is substantial dissatisfaction among young student affairs professionals with regard to their opportunities for advancement. Evans further indicates that a perception exists among young professionals that there is limited career mobility within the field.

Lorden (1998) suggests that administrators should seek alternate ways of providing formal opportunities for advancement, including internal promotions, new job titles, new responsibilities in another functional area, and other methods. She goes on to say, "The challenge that lies ahead is to identify and meet the needs of an increasingly diverse group of student affairs practitioners" (p. 214).

Working Conditions

Employment in student affairs sometimes represents less than ideal working conditions. Long hours, high expectations for availability to students, a volatile environment, turnover of students (about one-third of the students leave each year through graduation or other means), make stability and predictability difficult to achieve. In addition, normal organizational pressures make a new professional experience in student affairs challenging at best. New professionals work erratic hours, as their frontline responsibilities usually require them to adjust to student schedules. These sets of conditions can influence general feelings of satisfaction with personal lifestyles, and building a life separate from work may be difficult to achieve.

As professionals advance to mid-level management positions, some of the issues related to working conditions become more acute. For example, some studies indicate that women in mid-level positions in student affairs were significantly less satisfied with and committed to the profession of student affairs than were women in senior administrative positions (Bender, 1980; Blackhurst, Brandt, and Kalinowski, 1998; Blackhurst, 2000). There is some indication that as some professionals move up the administrative ladder, working conditions improve and then satisfaction increases.

Compensation

The issue of compensation is directly linked to working conditions experienced by professionals in student affairs. Given the working conditions just outlined, compensation becomes very important to some professionals, yet entry-level salaries in student affairs remain relatively low compared with other parts of the academy. Accurately assessing the compensation gap faced by student affairs is difficult at best. Confounding the issue is the lack of agreement within the profession of minimal qualifications for positions, lack of agreement regarding what job titles mean across institutions, and lack of a clear career path and credentialing process for student affairs professionals. This is particularly acute in generalist positions, where the job expectations are less clear and the criteria to determine what skills are necessary to do the work involved are more diffuse (Barr, 1990). "Although the ethos of higher education emphasizes intrinsic rewards, the hard work and low pay may lead many to pursue other attractive career options" (Lorden, 1998, p. 210).

Job Expectations and Evaluation

Defining the job that must be done is one of the greatest challenges in student affairs. Measuring success in student affairs seems often amorphous. Many supervisors, in fact, approach the definition of success like the Supreme Court defines pornography—they know it when they see it! Woodard and Komives (1990) suggest, however, that supervisors in student affairs should engage in formative staff evaluation by requiring staff to assess their own knowledge, skills, and attitudes as a method to help them meet their current and anticipated work challenges. In addition, evaluation should result in professional growth plans that ensure responsiveness and learning on the part of the professional staff member. Performance appraisal systems help staff members learn, grow, develop new competencies, and reduce ambiguity on the part of the employee. Such systems also assist staff members in moving forward in their individual career and education plans (Brown, 1988).

Supervision can make a difference. Dalton (2003) indicates that even in situations of demanding job expectations, supervisors can assist staff and prevent burnout if they can help employees do the following: fulfill the responsibilities for which they were hired, master the specific competencies necessary for success in assigned duties, understand and cope both professionally and personally with the culture and requirements of their work environment, and engage in continual learning (pp. 398–399). A tall order, to say the least, but one that has the potential to both attract and retain a diverse staff. Clear expectations and fair evaluations make a difference to staff, and a supervisor who provides both those clear expectations and continual supervision will create conditions whereby successful staff recruit other staff to the division.

Competition

Talented, diverse individuals are in demand both within and outside the academy. Both undergraduate and graduate students who may have considered higher education as a career are often diverted upon graduation to more lucrative opportunities in business and industry. Higher initial compensation, benefit packages, and greater clarity in career paths often make business and industry a more attractive alternative than higher education and student affairs. Seemingly more attractive career choices can also move staff members out of higher education.

In addition, competition occurs within the academy. Because most institutions have a very diffuse compensation system for staff with technical skills, for example, who receive higher compensation than those staff members serving in program development functions, competition within the academy is very strong. Talented, diverse individuals will be "poached" by other parts of the academy to meet needs, and such efforts may be successful if resources are available to such units that are not available in student affairs. Staff members who are diverse in some important dimension of their lives are clearly a desirable hire for other organizations both within and without higher education.

Commitment to the Profession

As indicated earlier, a number of professional staff members did not make an intentional decision to enter student affairs work. For a variety of reasons, such staff members found themselves as part of a student affairs organization. Many student affairs organizations assume that all professionals within a work unit share a set of common assumptions and beliefs about the profession. That is simply not true. There are variations in the level of commitment by student affairs staff to a specific position and to the profession of student affairs as a whole. For example, Blackhurst, Brandt, and Kalinowski (1998) indicate that women whose identities are linked to their administrative roles and who identify strongly with other colleagues at their institution experience significantly higher levels of organizational commitment than other women. To remain in the field, commitment appears to be an important variable.

Genuine Professional Development Opportunities

Sagaria and Johnsrud (1988) advocated that student affairs professionals should be encouraged to look beyond traditional vertical moves and see professional development as one avenue for personal and professional growth. For example, innovative courses such as the Harry Canon Administrative Fellowship Program at Northern

Illinois University provide opportunities for staff to stretch their skills and knowledge base with minimal investment of resources.

Involvement in professional organizations should also be encouraged and supported wherever possible, for such experiences also help staff members increase both their skills and knowledge base. NASPA, ACPA, and other professional organizations also provide intensive learning experiences for staff members interested in increasing their skills and competencies to prepare them for new roles and responsibilities.

All of these efforts are important, but the most effective professional growth opportunities often are the result of a well-developed, well-organized staff development program based on the campus and involving the staff in defining what is needed. Money is not the only answer, but innovative thinking about what could be done using local resources or individuals from other campuses can make a difference. Genuine staff development opportunities and continual opportunities for both formal and informal learning experiences can make a difference in both recruiting and retaining staff (Lorden, 1998).

Dimensions of Diversity

There are a number of dimensions of diversity that must be considered in developing student affairs professional staff members for the challenges of today and tomorrow. These dimensions of diversity among enrolled students include age, gender, minority status, disabilities, and sexual orientation.

Age

Edgerton (1999) reported that less than one in six of all current undergraduates in the United States fit the stereotype of "Joe College": eighteen to twenty-one years of age, white, male, and dependent on parents for financial support. Approximately 28 percent of all undergraduates in American colleges or universities are age twenty-five or older. Why does age matter when staffing is planned in student affairs? Consider the following: "An increasing proportion of today's students have been learning all their lives. Many have significant life experience before college (such as marriage, divorce, blending families, work, unemployment, paying bills, caring for relatives, coping with loss and travel abroad) and their life experiences have changed them. All of them continue to live lives outside of college itself. These trends familiar in the two-year college for decades, are now commonplace in four-year colleges and universities. Graduate and professional students have exhibited many of these characteristics all along" (National Association of Student Personnel Administrators, 2004, p. 7). Older students may need very different services than students of traditional age. Much can be learned about the unique perspectives and challenges of older students from professionals working in community colleges, in adult student learner offices (Kilgore and Rice, 2003) and from professionals working with graduate students (Pruitt-Logan and Isaac, 1995). For example, older students may need to work with individuals who have had broader life experiences than the majority of professionals completing master's level work in graduate preparation programs in student affairs. In fact, the aging of the American campus may require the profession to recruit older persons to student affairs and intentionally aid them in understanding the work of student affairs through staff development, mentoring, and further formal education.

Gender

In 1979, the number of women enrolled in American higher education equaled the enrollment of men for the first time (Woodard, Love, and Komives, 2000). By 2003, women represented 56 percent of students enrolled in American higher education (*Chronicle of Higher Education*, 2003). The change in the gender balance among students has influenced all aspects of higher education, including curriculum, policies, and programs (El-Khawas, 2003).

Title IX (U.S. Code secs, 1681–1686) specifically prohibits discrimination on the basis of sex in institutions of higher education except at some specifically designated institutional types. The influence of Title IX has been very strong and has shaped policies and procedures at American colleges and universities related to issues as diverse as sexual harassment and intercollegiate athletics (Barr, 2003). Although much progress has been made regarding sex discrimination, it is clear that more needs to be done.

"Unfortunately, in its own history the field of student affairs did not treat men and women equally. Deans of Women had to fight for equal recognition with Deans of Men; they fought even harder for the rights of women students" (Young, 2003, p. 100). Even today, student affairs organizations clearly have some challenges to meet regarding the issue of gender equity within the profession, particularly when it comes to the highest levels of responsibility in student affairs organizations. Walker, Reason, and Robinson (2003) indicate that gender "continues to be an important variable in hiring, promoting, and establishing salaries for student affairs professionals" (p. 147). Women still have not reached significant representation in senior student affairs positions at the larger and more prestigious institutions (Walker, Reason, and Robinson, 2003).

But the issue of gender does not just concern women. Although women now make up a majority of the entering class in American higher education and continue to graduate at a higher level than men (Woodard, Love, and Komives, 2000), this is cause for concern. Attention should be paid to the enrollment of male students and their rates of success in collegiate environments. Of particular concern is the enrollment by black men. Some studies have indicated that black men are less likely than black women to initially enroll in higher education and are more likely than women (if they do enroll) to experience a hostile or negative environment on campus (Cuyjet, 1997; Hopkins, 1977; Polite and Davis, 1999). It is clear that in general, there is a problem with enrollment, retention, and academic performance of college men, but it is most acute among at-risk men (African American, Native American, Latino, and low-income white males) (Kellom, 2004, p. 1).

These studies speak to the need for a diverse staff in student affairs, including both women and men and individuals from underrepresented minority groups. Reliance on graduate preparation programs for diversification of the professional student affairs staff may not be enough. Turrentine and Conley (2001) studied the enrollment in three types of graduate preparation programs granting master's degrees: administrative programs, counseling programs, and student personnel programs. Women comprised 65 percent of the enrollment in administrative programs, 78.8 percent of the enrollment in counseling programs, and 70.2 percent of the enrollment in student personnel programs. There is a dearth of men entering the student affairs profession through formal preparation programs, and this issue should be addressed. Both male and female students need positive reinforcement and positive role models as they learn and grow in higher education.

Minority Status

Three racial groups of students have received federal statutory protection against discrimination: African Americans, Hispanics, and Native Americans (El Khawas, 2003). Enrollment statistics and degree attainment in these protected classes do not indicate, however, that equality in higher education has been achieved (*Chronicle of Higher Education*, 2003).

Hispanic-Latino Students

Students who identify themselves as Latino or Hispanic represent a variety of different cultures, including Mexican American, Puerto Rican, Cuban American, and Central and South Americans (Torres, 2004). Within the larger group of Hispanic-Latino students, there are great differences in educational goals, socioeconomic status, family expectations, and post-graduate aspirations between and among these subgroups. Those differences are very real and must be

accounted for, as programs and services are developed for this growing student population.

There are also some commonalities that shape the work of student affairs with Latino-Hispanic student populations. For example,
the importance of family is a common theme for Hispanic-Latino
students. Ortiz indicates that "student services professionals who connect with Latino students, often serve as institutional mediators
between home and college experiences" (Ortiz, 2004, p. 91). To be
effective in working with Hispanic and Latino students, student
affairs staff members must extend their knowledge base about differences within this group, language barriers, cultural expectations, and
first-generational college issues.

Employing a staff that reflects at least some of the diversity
within the Hispanic-Latino student community would be an asset
to any student affairs organization but will be difficult to achieve.
Hispanic-Latino students are not well represented in student affairs
graduate preparation programs, with reports indicating that only 4.3
percent of the enrollment in administrative programs are Hispanic-
Latino; 3.9 percent of counseling students and 3.1 percent in student personnel programs are Hispanic-Latino (Turrentine and
Conley, 2001). New avenues for identification and recruitment of
qualified staff will need to be explored if rapid growth is sought in
Hispanic-Latino staff representation. In addition, it is essential that
all staff be willing to learn about such issues influencing this student
subpopulation so that they may translate that knowledge into programs that work to help students succeed.

African American Students

Students with African American identification have long been
underrepresented in traditional colleges and universities in the
United States. As noted earlier, the enrollment of African American
males is not growing at a significant rate and the statistics regarding
degree completion for this group are not encouraging. In 1997, enrollment of African American students in American colleges and

universities was 11 percent at the undergraduate level, 7.5 percent at the graduate level, and 7 percent at the professional school level. Adjustment to the collegiate environment may be a factor, with some studies indicating that prior interracial experiences are an important factor in the adjustment of African American students at primarily white institutions and that those African American students who have not had those experiences adjust better in historically black colleges and universities (Adan and Felner, 1995).

The issues faced by African American students are real and are very complex. The problem is how institutions and student affairs professionals can develop responses that work in mitigating some of these circumstances. One logical approach is to employ staff members who reflect and understand the African American experience in the United States and can provide assistance for African American students searching for their place in American higher education. The data indicate that specific goals also might prove difficult to achieve. African American students are only 10.8 percent of the enrollment in administrative preparation programs at the master's level, 11.0 percent of counseling programs, and 9.7 percent in student personnel programs (Turrentine and Conley, 2001).

African American students, as all students, flourish in environments characterized by both challenge and support. Without staff members prepared to provide both variables, success for African American students, particularly men, will be elusive (Cuyjet, 1997).

Native American Students

Although Native Americans are a protected class, as a group, they are the most overlooked and underrepresented minority group in American higher education. Tribal colleges have played a very important role in helping Native American students seek postsecondary educational opportunities. Beyond tribal colleges, however, the numbers of Native American students enrolled in American higher education are very small. To illustrate, Native Americans comprise more than 5 percent of the enrollment at eighty-five institutions, but only five of those institutions enroll more than five hundred Native American students. The total higher education enrollment statistics for Native American students are bleak, for even when enrollment in tribal colleges is counted, only three institutions across this nation enrolled more than a thousand Native American students on their campuses (Carney, 1999).

In order to serve this population, the concept of minorities must be expanded to include Native Americans. Institutions and student affairs professionals cannot overlook them in planning for multicultural activities, services, and programs on campuses. In addition, as a profession, student affairs must actively study the cultural differences within the Native American population that affect success in college for Native American students (McClellan, Fox, and Lowe 2004). A key link must involve student affairs professionals establishing relationships with tribal leaders to increase our own understanding and provide help to potential students. Finally, the profession must be intentional in encouraging Native American students to enter the field of student affairs; but we do not have a strong track record in that regard. Native American students are represented in master's degree preparation programs in very small numbers. Of the total enrollment in preparation programs, only .04 percent of students in administrative programs are Native American, 0.8 percent of counseling programs, and .07 percent of student personnel programs (Turrentine and Conley, 2001).

Asian American Students

Asian American students, although not a protected class from a statutory point of view, represent a growing percentage of enrollment at all levels in American higher education (Hune, 2002, p. 17). In fact, in 1997, Asian American students accounted for 6 percent of all undergraduate enrolled students in the United States, 22 percent of professional school enrollments, and nearly 5 percent of graduate school enrollments (Wilder, 2000). The growth in the professional school population is particularly significant. Yet the representation of Asian American students in graduate preparation programs in student affairs is very low. Only 1.5 percent of the enrollment in administrative preparation programs are Asian American, slightly less than 2 percent of counseling program enrollment, and 1.5 percent of student personnel preparation programs (Turrentine and Conley, 2001).

The differences between Asian American student subpopulations can be almost as great as those between Asian American students and students of other racial backgrounds. National origin, personal history, family and cultural traditions, lack of collegiate experience in the family, socioeconomic status, religion, and other factors all serve to subdivide the Asian American student population. However, in the late 1990s, Asian American students on many campuses banded together to work on issues of curriculum and support services for Asian American students.

Often the perception is that Asian American students are the high achievers within the campus community, which works to their disadvantage for they have many of the same hopes, dreams, problems, concerns, and aspirations as do other college students. Student affairs has lagged behind in recruiting Asian Americans to the profession and providing support for them once they enter the field. The Asian, Pacific Island Knowledge Community, within the National Association of Student Personnel Administrators, has become a visible way to highlight the specific issues of this subpopulation, but much more needs to be done. Student affairs professionals need to understand the nuances and the range of Asian American cultures entering American higher education. This may mean changes in graduate preparation curricula and staff development activities.

In addition, intentional efforts must be made to recruit more Asian Americans to the student affairs profession for these students, as all students, deserve positive role models of success as they struggle with the issues of identity development, career plans, and personal changes.

Students with Disabilities

Changes in statutes including the Americans with Disabilities Act (U.S. Code, Vol. 42. sec. 1202 et. seq.) and Section 504 of the Rehabilitation Act of 1973 (U.S. Code, Vol. 29, secs. 791–794) have provided the statutory authority for many individuals with disabilities (both seen and unseen) to access higher education. Many have come to colleges and universities who would never have enrolled prior to these two pieces of legislation. Sustaining these students within the educational environment has required new responses by institutions and student affairs professionals (Belch, 2000; Vickery and McClure, 1998). For many in student affairs, adjusting programs and services for students with disabilities presents both uncharted waters and unanticipated expense. Policy questions regarding what entity pays for what service, what services to provide, how to provide building access, program access, and housing accommodations have challenged the profession and higher education institutions. The answers to all of these questions are not yet clear, but it is clear that students with a wide range of disabilities will be enrolled in higher education from now on.

Reliance on student affairs graduate preparation programs to staff services for students with disabilities may not be enough. Specialized training and expertise is needed, and the profession needs to embrace professional staff with different experiences and backgrounds. In turn, such staff need to learn about the profession of student affairs and their role within it as they work with students with disabilities. New approaches need to be created in both services offered and developing the staff to provide such services. A staff that reflects diversity in all of its many dimensions, including disability, can serve as a powerful force for student success.

Sexual Orientation

Accurate data regarding the number of students currently enrolled in higher education who are gay, lesbian, bisexual, or transgender (GLBT) are difficult to establish. Despite progress in acceptance of differences in sexual orientation among students, concerns regarding discrimination and personal safety still plague some students, and there is reluctance to identify as a person with a different sexual orientation. Some estimate that as many as 7 percent of today's students are GLBT (Eyermann and Sanlo, 2002).

For some of these students, relationships with staff members who understand their life circumstances are essential to their success in the collegiate environment. The development of Safe Harbor programs on many campuses is but one response to the need for GLBT students to find a safe place to discuss concerns related to sexual orientation. At the professional organization level, the American College Personnel Association (ACPA) has provided leadership in recognizing the importance of GLBT staff on campus by establishing a standing committee to work on programs and services for this population. Other professional organizations have since developed similar structures to support GLBT professionals. However, on many campuses GLBT staff members face some of the same barriers as women in reaching the highest levels of responsibility in the organization.

Other Issues

There are of course many other dimensions of diversity that should be considered when building a student affairs staff prepared to work with the students of today and tomorrow. In addition to issues of age, gender, minority status, disability, GLBT concerns, and religious preference will be an issue on some campuses. On other campuses, particularly after the tragic events of September 11, 2001, national origin became an important area of diversity to consider when developing programs and services. On still other campuses, socioeconomic status of students is a diversity issue that must be addressed.

No matter how diversity among students is manifested, it is clear that institutions and students need to have student affairs staff members prepared to deal with the range of issues that accompany a more diverse student population. Intentional staff development programs and a climate of openness to new perspectives can aid student affairs staff members in learning about and responding to issues related to diversity. However, having colleagues who reflect the growing diversity of the student body can help professional staff understand the issues faced by students from diverse backgrounds from a new perspective. Finally, it must be remembered that diverse staff members cannot speak for everyone who shares their diversity, nor should they be expected to do so. They can, however, provide another perspective on problems and issues and an opportunity for other staff members to grow and continue to learn about differences.

Program Diversity

The evolving and ever-changing portfolio for student affairs provides yet another dimension of staff diversity to be considered in systematic planning for the future. The administrative responsibilities for student affairs units on many campuses have changed dramatically over the last fifty years. "New areas of responsibility are inevitable for student affairs in the future—because of organizational changes, the need to respond to new priorities, or the reality that student affairs is often the only area within the academy that will confront difficult issues" (Barr, 1990, p. 163). Specialized programs for substance abuse prevention, women's concerns, minority concerns, GLBT concerns, and disability services have often found their first home in a division of student affairs. Even programs that do not primarily serve specialized groups of students often find their home in student affairs, including health education, support programs for student athletes, service learning, and recreation.

Adoption of such new ventures requires employment of new staff with specialized training and expertise. It is not an issue new to student affairs. For example, on many campuses, integrating the health professionals from the student health center into the mainstream of student affairs has been an ongoing concern for years. Challenges abound, but so do opportunities to diversify the student affairs staff and bring new perspectives to the work of student affairs. In addition, some of these specialty areas reflect greater diversity with regard to minority status, disability, sexual orientation, and gender than does the traditional profession of student affairs. To illustrate, if intercollegiate athletics is part of the portfolio of student affairs, opportunities to increase the number of male staff (rightly or wrongly) are also increased. The same is true if campus safety or campus police are part of the division of student affairs. Dining and food services also bring opportunities to hire qualified diverse staff members at every level of the organization. Recreational and fitness programs may also bring individuals with diverse backgrounds and training to student affairs organizations. Multicultural student services are obvious units where intentionally diverse staff can be hired, but a caveat is in order. Multicultural services, or ethnic group services, should *not be the only* area within a division targeted for such hires. This list of units is merely illustrative of the opportunities that can be found for increased staff diversity through expansion of student affairs duties and responsibilities.

Suggestions for Action

Although it is true that some graduates of master's degree programs related to student affairs never intended to work in the field after graduation (Richmond and Sherman, 1991), the vast majority do have such intentions. The profession is, however, losing staff through attrition as documented by both Bender (1980) and Holmes, Verrier, and Chisholm (1983), with some estimates being as high as one-third of recent master's degree candidates graduating from such programs not entering the field.

Retaining diverse staff members is important to student affairs from several dimensions. First, as noted earlier, student affairs needs to serve a student body that grows more diverse with each passing year. Second, staff recruitment is costly in terms of both time invested by employed staff in the process and in actual dollars spent on the recruitment process. Third, leadership in student affairs must in the future reflect the diversity that is a part of American higher education. If the profession does not retain and help develop diverse staff, that may not be possible. The following are some strategies to be considered as the profession ponders the real dilemma of attracting and retaining a diverse staff.

1. *Understand the dimensions of the problem.* The leading professional organizations (NASPA and ACPA) should conduct research on the complexities of the issues involved in attracting and retaining a diverse staff. Once such research is conducted, the information that results should be made available to professionals in the field. In addition, these large professional organizations should encourage the specialty groups in student affairs, such as those associated with college unions, health services, orientation, and financial aid, to conduct similar research efforts. Such coordinated efforts might result in new insights on what it will take to attract and retain a diverse staff.

2. *Stop "hazing" new professionals.* There is a prevalent attitude in student affairs that current young staff members should do what now-established staff had to do when they entered the field. If anything has been learned about the changes in the student population, it is that they are different than previous generations of students. Logically, this means that young professionals will also embrace different values and ideas.

It is unrealistic to expect young professionals to just accept working conditions that could be improved. Student affairs administrators should begin to actively explore schemes for supervision and evaluation that account for irregular hours, compensatory time, and rewards other than pay. In addition, the profession should examine job expectations in terms of issues such as balance between personal and professional obligations. To do less means that the profession will lose a number of promising professionals.

3. *Develop and grow potential staff*. The enrollment statistics in master's degree programs for men and minority students are not encouraging, and currently, enrollment statistics in such programs for students with disabilities are difficult to quantify. The Minority Undergraduate Fellowship Program through NASPA is an example of a nationwide effort to encourage underrepresented groups of students to consider student affairs as an option. Recently, it began to include undergraduate students with disabilities. Although this is an important program, by itself it is not enough. Campuses also need to consider developing similar programs that are campus based. Consider, for example, an extended senior paraprofessional role for students who have completed the baccalaureate to expose them to the real day-to-day work of the profession. In addition to keeping diverse individuals affiliated with the institutions, such experiences can be powerful learning tools for students and staff alike. Such programs need to combine both work experience and exposure to the theories and assumptions and beliefs that undergird the work of student affairs.

Another alternative is to examine currently employed staff who may be underemployed in the current job assignments in the division. Sometimes someone who is employed as an administrative assistant, for example, could profit from additional responsibilities to determine if a career choice in student affairs is a viable alternative for their future. The key to "growing" staff members is being active in the process of identifying potential candidates from diverse backgrounds who are already students or staff members at the institution and encouraging such individuals to carefully examine the field of student affairs.

4. *Clearly define job expectations*. Each administrator should work very carefully to define success in specific job assignments in student affairs. Staff members who clearly understand what the performance expectations are for a position are likely to flourish. Be clear and direct regarding job expectations during the hiring process

and through continual feedback during employment. When the role and function of a position is unclear, staff become uncertain and tentative. And it follows that uncertain and tentative staff are likely to leave the field of student affairs.

5. *Continually recruit.* Recruitment of diverse, qualified staff is an ongoing process. The effective student affairs administrator recruits even when there are no positions available at their institution. Identify diverse new professionals who have promise and keep in touch with them on an informal basis. Offer to work with them on projects and programs. When a position becomes available, they might be interested in applying because they know you and your institution. Or if they are personally not interested, they may know of someone else from a diverse background whom they could encourage to apply for an open position. In addition, by continually recruiting, the astute student affairs professional can learn a great deal and personally grow and develop from association with talented young professionals.

6. *Fight the compensation battle.* Although progress has been made in raising the level of compensation for student affairs professionals, much more needs to be done to meet the competitive demands for diverse staff both within and without the institution. The effective student affairs administrator does not assume that the compensation battle cannot be won. Develop data that support increased compensation by providing comparable information from like institutions. In addition, the development of other reward systems (such as covering moving expenses, child care, tuition reduction for employees and family members, paying for professional development, or paying professional dues) for employees should be considered. The compensation battle never is fully won, but the well-prepared administrator can make a difference in this arena.

Professional associations should also take leadership in this important area by conducting well-documented salary surveys on a regular basis and making that information available to professionals in the field.

7. *Explore new ways of working.* Do not close off opportunities to discuss new and innovative ways of working with professional staff members. Job sharing, telecommuting one day a week, academic year appointments, working non-traditional hours, and a whole host of other approaches should be considered and may be attractive to staff. Although it is difficult to implement such programs in a regulated human resources environment, do not assume it cannot be done. Develop a strategy for retaining a staff member and seek input from human resources in the process. Professionals in human resources can be of great help in determining alternatives for employment that still meet regulatory requirement and institutional policies.

8. *Help specialty staff members understand student affairs.* Student affairs include many individuals without formal training in student affairs but who have a deep understanding of their professional specialty area. If efforts are not made to link such specialty staff to the work and mission of student affairs, the potential for disengagement of such staff is very real.

Therefore, the leadership across the division of student affairs must articulate the goals for student affairs work; define the knowledge base, skills, and competencies needed by all staff; and provide intentional staff development opportunities for specialty staff to gain those skills if they need them. The division will be stronger for it because individual staff members will feel more connected to the mission and see the link between their specialty area and the work of student affairs.

9. *Share knowledge.* Student affairs staff members should be encouraged to share their knowledge about students with key constituency groups both within and without the institution. Too often student affairs staff are diffident about their knowledge and skills. Staff members must understand the changes in the student body and translate those changes into meaningful information for their faculty and staff colleagues on campus. If research is conducted, share the results. If faculty want to know about the changes in students, for example, volunteer to present to a department or a school. Such opportunities are but another way to highlight the skills and

competencies of all staff members and have them be seen as experts on students within the campus community.

Even though staff members are busy, such efforts can increase the knowledge base of others and have the potential to make the learning environment more amenable to the ever-changing student body. Basic to this recommendation is a commitment to helping staff retain professional competence through internal and external intentional staff development activities.

10. *Celebrate and appreciate staff contributions*. Each supervisor in student affairs needs to identify large and small ways to thank and show appreciation, on a regular basis, for staff contributions to the work of student affairs. Gestures that may be seen as insignificant to the supervisor may have great meaning for staff. Handwritten notes, public words of praise, e-mails, a drop-in office visit, or a phone call expressing appreciation can make a world of difference to a hardworking staff member.

Reward systems are also helpful in concretely letting staff know that their individual contribution makes a difference. Although such efforts do not replace adequate compensation packages, each is important as part of the effort to retain qualified, competent staff.

Summary

The problem of attracting and retaining diverse individuals in the profession of student affairs is a complex one and will not be easily solved. But it must be addressed if we are to fulfill our obligations to students and institutions of higher education. Some strategies have been presented in this chapter, but this is just the beginning.

Professional associations and practitioners need to examine the issue of attracting and retaining a diverse staff very carefully and develop strategies that work with the unique campus environments where they work. Creativity and commitment are both essential. This is not a problem that can be ignored or expected to solve itself without intentional effort. To do less invites failure for both students and the institutions that the profession serves.

5

How Do Sources of Revenue Affect Student Affairs?

Student affairs administrators are responsible for many essential programs and departments on their campuses. If they are going to be successful in their work, they must be effective in administering the budget for their division. These budgets can be quite large and often include very diverse activities and functions. Moreover, the sources of revenue for the various services may be quite different, depending upon the nature of the campus, state regulations, endowment support, and the institution's history and traditions. Student affairs administrators are responsible for securing financial resources, allocating them in a manner consistent with institutional priorities and remaining accountable for the funds they oversee. Senior student affairs officers are also participants in the institutional budget process and should not only be persuasive in advocating financial support for the programs they represent but also knowledgeable contributors to the overall budget decision-making process of their institution.

The question of what the revenue sources for student affairs should be is often debated within the profession. Should the various programs and services in student affairs be funded from the regular institutional budget, from mandatory student fees, from user fees, or from other sources? Does the source of funding have an impact on the success of the student affairs programs or upon the manner in which student affairs administrators perform their duties? Should student affairs leaders advocate a specific source of funding for the programs they administer? These are important questions for student affairs leaders to consider as they work to improve their programs and services.

In this chapter, the fiscal responsibilities of student affairs administrators within the broad context of higher education will be discussed; issues related to the various revenue sources for student affairs will be reviewed; the funding debate within student affairs will be presented; and suggestions for action regarding fiscal management in student affairs will be offered.

The Changing Fiscal Scene in Higher Education

Student affairs administrators are more effective when they understand the ever-increasing complexities that they'll encounter as they pursue sources of revenue for student affairs.

Funding as a Volatile Issue

There is perhaps some irony that at the same time the American system of higher education is the envy of the world, it is also the subject of virulent criticism and scrutiny at home (Bok, 1992). Students and scholars from dozens of other countries compete vigorously for the chance to study at American universities, and at home, state legislators, governors, national commissions, and the general public continue to criticize the academy (for example, Shuman, 1997; Smith, 1990; Wilshire, 1990; Aronowitz, 2000; Bok, 2003). Even though access to higher education has been greatly expanded, there is increasing concern about quality in undergraduate education, and several state legislatures have required public institutions to conduct assessments to provide evidence of what students have learned during their period of enrollment. With over fifteen million students enrolled in American colleges and universities, there is increasing concern about what students are learning, how much it costs, and who should pay for these costs.

Earning the Public's Trust

The former Harvard President Derek Bok argued that higher education needs to "reclaim the public trust" (1992). Misuse of public funds, dishonest reporting of research results, paying scant attention to undergraduate teaching at research universities, and allowing abuses in big-time intercollegiate athletics have all contributed to a loss of public confidence. A national report (Wingspread Group, 1993) suggested that the "withdrawal of public support for higher education can only accelerate as students, parents, and taxpayers come to understand that they paid for an expensive education without receiving fair value in return" (p. 2).

Technology and Entrepreneurship

Among the greatest challenges to traditional colleges and universities in 2005 is the new technology, which has changed the ways students learn, professors teach, and institutions are organized. The Internet, in particular, has profoundly changed economies, markets, products, services, consumer behavior, and of course, education (Drucker, 2002). Moreover, existing colleges and universities face increased competition from for-profit institutions (Blumenstyk and Farrell, 2003; Borrego, 2001; Burd, 2003). The new *online universities* (for example, Sperling, 2000) have provided new access to higher education for large numbers of citizens, a situation almost unimagined ten years ago. Higher education administrators have had to become much more entrepreneurial in recent years (for example, Breneman and Taylor, 1996; Clark, 1998), and college presidents and other senior leaders in both public and private institutions are expected to spend significant time in efforts to raise private funds. This new financial pressure has caused some to warn about the dangers of commercializing higher education (Slaughter and Leslie, 1997; Shuman, 1997; Gould, 2003; Bok, 2003). As governing boards and presidents try to streamline their institutions, such options as outsourcing and contracting for services also have become increasingly common (Bartem, 2001; Kirp, 2002).

Increased Dependence on External Funding

Some large, public research universities, such as the University of Virginia and the University of Michigan, now receive less than a quarter of their total revenues from direct state appropriations (White, 2003; Zemsky, 2003; Mills and Barr, 1990), causing them to be increasingly dependent on the success of their faculty in the competition for research grants and upon their own entrepreneurial activities. Finally, state appropriations for public institutions have been significantly reduced in some states, and political opposition to higher tuition for students has become much more strenuous.

More Public Scrutiny

American higher education in 2005 is an accurate reflection of its society: it is huge, expensive, accessible, ambitious, restless, anxious, and under attack. While it is undergoing significant change from within, it is facing serious challenges from outside. Students can choose among many options—community colleges, for-profit institutions, online colleges, liberal arts colleges, research universities, and many others—as the ways education is delivered continue to expand. Perhaps most important, federal and state agencies and the general public are scrutinizing the costs of both public and private higher education very carefully, and this financial scrutiny places great pressures on administrative leaders in colleges and universities. What higher education institutions do is no longer shielded from public view; the public wants to know what it is getting for its money. This situation is directly affecting student affairs, its financial resources, and its expenditures.

The Student Affairs Budgetary Climate

Fiscal Constraints

With all the turmoil in higher education and the increased public scrutiny given to how colleges and universities expend their funds, it is no surprise that student affairs leaders are experiencing similar issues concerning their budgets. Schuh (1993, p. 49) stated that "fiscal policy, constraints, and conditions have all had a profound effect on programs, services, learning opportunities, and activities developed and offered in the student affairs division." Trow (1995, p. 15) characterized the current budgetary climate of student affairs as "tentative, cautiously optimistic, competitive, depressing, or uncertain. The current situation in higher education reflects increasing calls for accountability, outcomes assessment, and governmental regulations and reporting requirements that place additional demands on already slim budgets."

Demands for Additional Services

At the same time that there are decreasing institutional and state resources for budgets and increased scrutiny placed upon costs, student affairs administrators are also being expected to provide additional support services to students. For example, perhaps due to the increased stress experienced by young people before they enter college, demands for medical and psychological support for students have increased substantially (Young, 2003). Woodard (2001, p. 256) sees this trend continuing, as he asserts that "most observers see a continuing pattern of turbulence, dissatisfaction, cost saving measures, increased productivity, cost saving technology, and the generation of new and increasing sources of revenue." Student affairs leaders are strongly committed to assisting students but are finding it increasingly difficult to meet students' needs with available institutional resources. The level of competition for resources within institutions has become intense, necessitating student affairs administrators to become strong advocates for their budgetary needs.

Need to Secure More Resources

Good student affairs leaders know they will not be able to achieve success unless they are effective in securing resources, allocating them wisely, and managing these resources prudently. As Woodard argued, "the budget is the single most important work tool the student affairs administrator uses in developing and implementing activities to meet agreed-upon program activities and outcomes" (2001, p. 245). In the current climate of restricted resources, it is clear that student affairs leaders must redesign roles, procedures, and organizational structures if they are going to meet new demands (Kotter, 1995). Student affairs administrators need to have strong budgetary and planning skills, as financial pressures on their divisions increase.

Declining Institutional Sources

Williamson and Mamarchev (1990, p. 200) identified various forces that have contributed to the decline of institutional support for student affairs; among these are competition for institutional resources, shifting priorities, a decline of external resources, and rising student consumerism. They also argue that "expertise in the financial arena is not a focal point of most student affairs operations, but it can no longer be avoided if the student affairs mission is to continue safely into the 21st century." Furthermore, some observers have noted that "the reputation that student affairs officers have, especially among their colleagues on the business side of their institution, is that they do not manage their resources well, and that it is not uncommon to find a general lack of experience and expertise in financial management among student services professionals" (Schuh and Rickard, 1989, p. 461; Pembroke, 1985, p. 101). Student affairs administrators are just as likely as others in the academy to be vulnerable to the "common pitfalls" (Barr, 2002) of budget management: over-estimating revenue, postponing a problem, failing to ask for help, failing to identify hidden costs, failing to plan for the end, failing to identify multiyear consequences, failing to understand implications for others, and assuming the good times will continue.

Making Good Fiscal Management a Priority

The obstacles to effective budget management in student affairs are numerous, but as Ern (1993, p. 453) suggested, "No one has ever said that maintaining the rigor and handling the strong emotions associated with budgeting and planning would be easy. . . . student affairs professionals, especially chief student affairs officers must take fiscal management seriously; to do less invites failure." He further asserted that "the fact is that there are two enduring institutional cultures, (academic and service) so do not fight the situation. Educate your colleagues on the faculty about what student affairs does and how it interrelates with their work." Securing new resources, maintaining current assets, and allocating resources is one of the most competitive and stressful aspects of college and university administration, and student affairs administrators must learn how to be persuasive advocates and frugal managers within this highly competitive climate.

New Accountability Schemes

Confronted with such changing financial systems as cost centers, zero-based budgeting, formula budgeting, program budgeting, responsibility-centered budgeting, line item budgeting, and total quality-management budgeting, senior student affairs administrators face the same dilemma their colleagues in academic, research, business, and development affairs face—how to adapt their needs to the particular budget system in vogue at the time. This problem has been especially true in state universities in the past twenty years, as legislatures and statewide boards have mandated new allocation and accountability processes, often based upon entirely new budgetary systems. Whatever the system, student affairs administrators must become effective in finding resources, allocating them wisely, assessing the impact of their allocation decisions, and accounting for these resources. This has resulted in some lively discussion about funding within the profession.

The Funding Debate Within Student Affairs

Non-traditional Sources of Support

As pressures have mounted to provide additional services and to streamline or reduce other services, it was inevitable that non-traditional sources of revenue would assume a more prominent role in the funding of student affairs. Competition to fund academic programs from the general institutional budget has become so intense that very few, if any, colleges and universities are now able to meet all the demands from faculty, students, and external groups. Thus, for many of the programs within student affairs, institutions have increasingly turned toward student fees, grants, external fundraising, and outsourcing for support (for example, Rhoades, 1995; Jackson, 2000; Schuh, 1993; Penney and Rose, 2001; Kirp, 2002; Bartem, 2001). This has caused a good deal of discussion within the student affairs profession about how programs should be supported. It has also resulted in some controversy about the appropriate use of various student fees (Hebel, 2002; Carnevale, 2001).

On many campuses, of course, financial support for student affairs programs and services comes from more than one source; it is common that student fees will support some services, student rents will support some activities, and the general fund of the institution will support others. Some institutions may adopt *user fees* for the support of some services that are considered important to certain students, but not all (such as child-care programs). As institutional budgets continue to become tighter, and demands for new academic programs become more intense, it is clear that more colleges and universities are turning to student fees as a source for facilities, programs, and services.

Student Fees or Direct Institutional Support?

Receiving direct support for student affairs programs and services may be interpreted as an indication of an institutional commitment to these programs. Student affairs programs at such institutions may be viewed as an important part of the core mission of the institution.

If student affairs is viewed as a vital part of the educational program of the campus, then senior student affairs leaders will compete for institutional resources with their academic, research, development, and administrative colleagues. Advocates suggest that this approach enables student affairs to be better understood and appreciated and ensures that it is a fully accepted partner in the institution's overall educational program. For those who believe in close cooperation and collaboration between academic and student affairs, this approach to securing financial resources may be especially important.

It may be argued by advocates of this position that when student affairs programs and services are funded from student fees, this reinforces the idea that student affairs is not a vital part of the campus and can be disregarded as a mere "sideline" activity, funded by the students, and outside the main academic arena of the institution. Others might assert that funding student affairs programs and services from required student fees places an unfair or discriminatory financial burden on many students and may distort the perceived costs of attending the institution. Critics of the student fee approach to funding student services may assert that it may cause resentment toward student affairs because of its "privileged funding position" and may even result in accusations that student affairs leaders manipulate students in order to obtain their support for new or increased student fees.

Funding student affairs functions from student fees may affect access to various services if there is a user fee involved. Such a situation can obviously be discriminatory against lower-income students. Even when required student fees support a service or a program (such as a student health center or mental health program), there may be additional user fees, and such fees may discourage some students who need the service from receiving it.

Do Student Fees Ensure Program Stability?

Support of student affairs programs and services from required student fees may also be interpreted as the most successful way to secure resources. Advocates of this approach argue that student affairs will never be able to compete on an equal basis with core academic and research programs and thus need the financial security that can only come from student fees. Moreover, advocates of this approach may assert that being funded from student fees makes their programs and services more responsive to student needs, because they are directly accountable to the students who are funding them. Funding student affairs programs and services from student fees may be viewed as a form of financial protection from institutional cutbacks during difficult budget years (so long as student enrollment remains steady). Thus, this approach may be viewed as giving student affairs a degree of financial independence and stability not enjoyed by other areas of the campus. If student affairs programs and services are among the most vulnerable to cutbacks during times of financial crisis, it can be argued that the student fee approach is quite attractive.

Who Decides Student Fees?

In some states, various student fees have been levied not by the institutional governing board or the campus president, but by the state legislature. Of course in some cases, these legislatively imposed fees have been recommended to the legislature by these same governing boards and presidents. At independent colleges and universities, when a student fee is established, it is the result of action taken by the governing board, usually with the recommendation of the president to do so. Sometimes some form of consent from the students themselves is sought, especially when facilities (such as new recreation centers) are constructed. Some student affairs leaders (and their presidents) may believe that the only realistic way to acquire new facilities, programs, and support for student affairs in such difficult budgetary times is through student fees. Especially in state colleges and universities, legislatures are increasingly reluctant to fund programs, services, and facilities that they do not view as part of the core academic program. The situation may be similar in some private institutions as well, as the governing board may decide that the only way to build and support new student affairs programs is through student fees or through substantial gifts from donors.

Some Institutional Examples

As illustrations of the varied funding arrangements for student affairs, a few institutional examples follow: at Texas A & M University, the total student affairs annual budget exceeds $70 million. Of this amount, less than 5 percent comes from state-appropriated funds. Income from student housing rents and various student fees comprise the overwhelming portion of the budget. At the universities of Memphis, Illinois, and Georgia, well over half of the student affairs budget now is generated by a variety of fees. However, at Miami University in Ohio, student fees comprise considerably less than half of the total student affairs budget. At Southern Methodist University, a private institution, student fees only comprise about 2 percent of the overall student affairs budget. But at other private institutions, such as Bowdoin College, the University of Miami, and the University of Southern California, student fees comprise a much higher percentage of the total student affairs budget. Although there is considerable variation in how student affairs programs, services, and facilities are supported, the trend toward student fees is clear (Rhoades, 1995).

Source of Funds Not as Important as Leadership

The debate about this issue within student affairs has often focused on the source of financial support: Should the student affairs budget come from student fees or from the regular institutional budget? Some student affairs leaders have assumed that their effectiveness as financial managers is dependent upon the source of support for their programs. In this process, they may have misconstrued their roles as financial managers, acting as if the source of funds for their division determine or restrict their role. Regardless of the source of funds, senior student affairs officers should assume a leadership role in institution-wide fiscal affairs.

Senior student affairs officers have the responsibility to secure financial support for their division's programs, services, and facilities.

As described earlier in this chapter, the challenges they face in this regard are considerable, as institutional resources dwindle, student demand for services increase, and as competition for resources becomes more intense. This is a critical issue for student affairs leaders that demands their full attention.

Suggestions for Action

The following suggestions are offered for consideration by the profession.

1. *Student affairs officers should become experts about their institution's budgets and become knowledgeable contributors to the process.* If they focus their efforts only on the sources of financial support for their own divisional programs, services, and facilities, they may find themselves closed out of the ongoing, established institutional budgeting process. The sources of support are really not the issue for student affairs administrators—being a full contributing and participating member of the institutional budget process is the key. If senior student affairs officers choose not to be a vital part of the institutional budgeting team, they are falling into the "trap of sole reliance on fees!" There is no substitute for the senior student affairs officer being a regular part of the institutional management team, whether this is accomplished via membership on the president's cabinet or the institutional budget committee.

It may be quite tempting for student affairs leaders to attach their futures to support via student fees, thinking that by doing so they are establishing a secure and solid future for their programs. But by doing this, they may find themselves becoming excluded from a significant role on the institution's management team. This can seriously jeopardize the success of the student affairs division.

2. *Senior student affairs officers should be strong and persuasive advocates for their division's programs, whatever the sources of support*

may be. The major portion of the student affairs budget may come from student fees, but the senior student affairs officer still needs to be a full participant in the institution's budget decision-making process, along with the senior academic, research, development, and business officers. If they are not viewed by their presidents and their other senior administrative colleagues as competent, well-informed financial managers, then their voices will not be heard. Eventually, this will result in a diminished role for student affairs programs and services within the institution.

3. *Student affairs leaders should understand that they will have to be active entrepreneurs for their division by seeking and securing funds from external sources*. It is no longer realistic for student affairs leaders to assume that all of their needs for programs and services can be met through the traditional institutional budget. As with their colleagues in academic affairs, it will be expected that student affairs officers will generate a significant portion of their needed funds from sources outside the institution. This will also require student affairs officers to become effective stewards of these funds.

4. *Student affairs leaders should become very familiar with trends in outsourcing of services and programs, both within their division and within the total institution*. With the rapid technological "flattening of the world" (Friedman, 2005), it is highly likely that colleges and universities will be following the lead of corporations in seeking more efficient and less costly ways of conducting their business. Student affairs leaders will benefit by becoming knowledgeable about this movement and by exploring better ways to provide services.

5. *Student affairs leaders should "follow the money" on their campuses*. They should know that the institutional budget is the most important statement of priorities on the campus. Their focus, of course, should continue to be upon student learning, but they must understand that the educational services and programs they want for their students will only be possible if adequate funds are secured. It is the responsibility of senior student affairs officers to see that this happens.

Summary

Colleges and universities are facing serious financial challenges in 2006, and at the same time, students are demanding more services and programs. Greater public scrutiny is also being given to institutions of higher education. As technology continues to change the ways education is delivered, competition for resources within institutions has become very rigorous. Student affairs leaders are just as passionate about their programs and services as their academic, development, research, and administrative colleagues are about theirs. If student affairs leaders are to achieve their goals on their campus, it is essential that they become expert fiscal managers, articulate advocates for their programs, creative resource procurers, and knowledgeable contributors to their institution's overall budget processes.

6

What Is the Role of Student Affairs in Non-traditional Educational Settings?

The ways students engage in educational opportunities have changed dramatically during the last three decades. For example, a student can enroll, participate in classes, conduct research, take examinations, use the library, and graduate through online access, without ever having to set foot on the traditional college campus. Or a student can enroll in a traditional institution and then participate in an internship, engage in a cooperative education program, study abroad, participate in other educational opportunities, and be removed from campus for a substantial amount of time during his or her period of enrollment. Or a student who is enrolled as a full-time student on campus can take some core courses online in a virtual classroom, via streaming video, or through teleconferencing, because of the convenience of the class schedule and the availability of the course. Or a student can take virtually all courses at an off-campus center located in close proximity to home and never come to the main campus. Finally, some students in very remote locations can engage in paper-and-pen correspondence courses.

In all of these settings and others, students enroll in public, private, two- and four-year institutions and proprietary schools. The pathways to educational experiences for students are many, change rapidly, and serve diverse student populations with a range of both needs and wants. The future holds a number of possibilities, as technology advances and student sophistication in alternate means of education grows. It is an exciting time to be engaged in the educational enterprise, but the student affairs profession has not yet clearly defined its role in this ever-changing range of possibilities for instruction and education.

Defining the role of student affairs in non-traditional educational settings is critical to the future of the profession. A number of questions will need to be answered. What services and programs can and should be provided to students regardless of how they are accessing their educational opportunities? What are the possibilities and the pitfalls for student affairs in serving the distance learner? What should be the role of student affairs in developing programs involving study abroad, internships, and cooperative education? What are the limits inherent in using technology to provide direct student services and programs? This set of questions is merely illustrative of the complex set of issues that must be answered by student affairs and higher education as the educational environment shifts and changes.

Students also can and should have some reasonable expectations for services provided by educational institutions, as outlined in *Promoting Reasonable Expectations* (Miller, Bender, Schuh, and Associates, 2005), based on a work commissioned and published by the National Association of Student Personnel Administrators (NASPA) (Kuh, Lyons, Miller, and Trow, 1995). Among these expectations are the following: "making services available by competent personnel at convenient times and locations in a cost-effective and efficient manner" (Kuh, Lyons, Miller, and Trow, 1995). Rapid changes in technology, transportation, and the economy are creating new settings where and when such services might be offered and under what conditions. Those new settings create major challenges and opportunities for the student affairs profession.

This chapter will provide an overview of the three major types of non-traditional educational settings for students today and will highlight some of the programs and services currently being provided to students. In addition, the issues involved in providing student services and programs in such environments will be high-lighted. Finally, the chapter will conclude with some suggestions for consideration by the student affairs profession as the future of education unfolds.

Three general types of non-traditional educational settings are explored in this chapter. The first setting focuses on the use of some form of technology to provide student access to education. A second non-traditional setting involves bringing the academic program to the student at a site located in geographical proximity to where the student lives or works. The final non-traditional setting explored in this chapter involves the individual student leaving the campus to study in another country or to participate in a work-learning experience in business, industry, government, or social service. Each of these settings brings unique questions and challenges regarding what kinds of student affairs program, services, and support should be provided to participating students.

Technology

Kinley (2001) indicates that although forms of distance education have been around since the 1800s, recently Internet technology has fostered rapid growth and development in distance learning. The rapid growth of technology as a learning tool brings many issues to higher education. In fact, a poll conducted by the North Central Association of Colleges and Schools found that university presidents felt that accountability and expansion of distance education would be the two factors having the greatest impact on the regulatory activities of accrediting association (DeAlva, 2000).

Students

The development of technology has also contributed to changes in the characteristics of students engaged in distance education. Kruger (2003) states that "enrollment in distance education, or virtual classes, is dominated by campus-based students" (p. 23). If this is true, then the assumptions made by Blimling and Whitt (1999, p. 7) that students engaged in distance education were primarily older, part-time, working people who do not have the opportunity to attend a traditional campus should be carefully reexamined. There are some indications that whether students are of traditional age or not, they are prone to "shop" for courses that best accommodate their personal schedules and circumstances and then transfer earned online credits to institutions where they will earn their degree (Johnstone, Ewell, and Paulson, 2002). The question for student affairs is what services (if any) do these online students want and need? Some of that answer is clear and some is still very murky.

Administrative Core Functions

"Higher education increasingly is becoming reliant on technology both in and out of the classroom" (Woodard, Love, and Komives, 2000, p. 27). For example, a number of core administrative functions, including some in student affairs, have successfully been fully or partially transferred to the Internet. Web-based campus tours, application processes, class registration, financial aid applications, financial aid awards, student billing, payments, student financial records, and scheduling of events for student organizations are common at many colleges and universities. It is clear that students and their families have transferred their experience with online businesses, banking, and other e-commerce to higher education. This experience has created a growing expectation for access to basic institutional information and services twenty-four hours a day, seven days a week.

Administrative core functions on the Web often serve both distance learners and students residing on campus. To illustrate, the University of Minnesota has developed and implemented a paperless financial aid office, allowing financial aid applicants and recipients to perform all transactions without a single piece of paper. This innovation has had at least three positive outcomes: administrative cost savings, reduction in processing time, and freeing of staff time to directly respond to students via telephone, the Web, e-mail, or in person. Minnesota provides an important lesson in the use of technology: it can help improve direct and indirect services for all students both on and off campus. However, the speed of technology also has a downside. This age of instant communication via e-mail, cell phone, chat rooms, and fax has raised expectations by students and families for a quick response from the institution. When such systems have been implemented, major adjustments have been required on the part of the institution and student affairs professionals. In addition, although resources have been channeled into technology and the technological competence of staff has increased, still the distance learner remains isolated from the individual and personal support provided to on-campus students.

Student affairs is clearly coming quite late to the distance learning environment. Kruger (2003) states that "distance education programs are building and creating sophisticated student services components to complement their online course offerings" (p. 23). He indicates that the breadth of these services goes far beyond the administrative core functions previously described and includes functions related to academic advising, orientation, community building, counseling, career development, mentoring, and job placement. The following are examples of such programs.

Academic Advising

Providing access to quality academic advising to distance learners via the Internet is an enormous challenge. Kerr (2002) indicates that online advising services need to provide access to both information and human resources and must help focus distance learners toward their educational goals. For example, Penietz (1997) found that academic advising was deemed the most important student service for students enrolled in community college distance education programs. A variety of technology-based academic-advising approaches are described by Sotto (2003). These include videoconferencing, computer chats, and e-mail. For any long-distance academic-advising system to be effective, however, the distance learner must have easy access to basic information on policies and procedures.

Access by the distance learner to assessment tests must be provided. In addition, the results of such tests must be available and interpreted to the academic adviser working with the distance learning student. New innovations have also occurred. For example, Patankar (1998) describes a Web-based Academic Counseling Expert (ACE) system that supplements online or telephone advising by faculty or trained academic advisers. Kerr (2002) states that to be effective, academic advising for distance learners must be rethought and redesigned. Just introducing technology to a face-to-face system, however, is not enough. He goes on to indicate that the academic-advising system for distance learners must be easily accessible to students at all times, must be continually and accurately updated, and must provide links to the most up-to-date rules, regulations, and course offerings. Easily accessible information also needs to be provided regarding other sources of help on campus that may be reached via e-mail or telephone.

There are some inherent limitations in distance academic advising. What is often missing, for example, are the subtle verbal and nonverbal cues and clues given by students in face-to-face advising sessions. These clues help advisers probe deeper and make the exploration of options more complete. However, Sotto (2000) indicates that advances in technology may be addressing such issues, citing a teleconferencing system described by Menlove, Hansford, and Lignugaris-Kraft (2000) that delivers voice and video advising for preservice teacher education students in remote geographical areas.

Although progress has been made in providing academic advising through the use of technology, much more work needs to be done. Part of that work should focus on providing assistance to the distance learner in preparing for virtual advising sessions and assisting the distance learner in acquiring the skills to follow through on referrals and research.

In addition, to be effective, distance learners must be able to take the risk to talk about their personal aspirations with an unknown person via technology. Concurrently, the institution must be flexible in dealing with distance learners as they attempt to negotiate a complex system of rules, regulations, and expectations from far away.

A number of online resources can help inform the discussion regarding providing academic advising via technology. *The Mentor*, for example, is a free online publication about academic advising in higher education focused on current issues and problems. Other resources include The Penn State eLion academic-advising demonstration site (eliondemo.oas.psu.edu/general/welcome_advisers.html) and the University of Delaware's Web Initiatives site (www.mis. udel.edu/main/webinits/). These sites are helpful in providing a perspective on the issues involved. In addition, the National Academic Advising Association (NACADA) provides valuable information on remote academic advising through the NACADA Technology in Advising Commission (www.psu.edu/dus/ncta/linkspec.htm# distance). Clearly, any move to use technology in academic advising should be carefully planned and evaluated to determine both the intended and unintended consequences of such an evolving process.

Career Development and Job Placement

Technological advances have already been a boon to the detailed and complicated world of campus career development centers across the nation. The use of technology has been particularly helpful in providing information to students about internships, full- and part-time employment opportunities, information about prospective employers, on-campus interview scheduling, and application processes for graduate and professional schools. Although distance learners can take only limited advantage of on-campus interviewing opportunities, a well-designed and maintained career services Web site can be very valuable to the distance learner.

Rayman (1993) predicted that five major areas in career services would be positively affected by technology, including electronic storage, retrieval, and transmission of credentials; computer-administered and interpreted assessments; video interviewing; computer-assisted career guidance, voice mail and other telephone technologies (p. 102). His predictions were accurate, and each of the innovations mentioned support both distance learners and on-campus students.

However, for any student (distance learner or not) there are a dizzying array of Web sites available on career matters. A recent Internet search for career counseling information, for example, yielded over 1,300,000 possible hits. The choices range from for-profit, commercial sites operated by corporations such as the *Wall Street Journal* (www.wsj/careerdev.org/) to individuals offering career counseling and assessment over the Internet. In addition, most college and university career services use the Internet to provide at least basic information to students regarding career services.

A new challenge for student affairs may be in providing sufficient information and general advice to both students in remote locations and on campus about the problems and pitfalls of career counseling over the Internet. Making distance learners aware of the need for accreditation and licensing of the provider, the ethical standards involved, and what questions to ask may be among the most important assistance institutions can give to the distance learner in this arena.

Job placement services, résumé depositories, and other sites that provide potential links between prospective employers and potential employees all abound on the Internet. Monster.com, for example, is among the most visible of such sites that are available to students both on and off campus. The issues involved in the provision of such services are very similar to those involved in career counseling over the net. Distance learners, in particular, may be less aware of the ethical standards that should govern the interactions between job seekers and potential employers. Part of the responsibility of an institution is to make sure that all students, whatever their method of accessing educational opportunities, have access to basic information to aid them in making informed choices about Internet-based services. For example, an institution could provide a link from the campus Web site to the National Association of Colleges and Employers (NACE) site where the Principles for Professional Conduct for career services and employment professionals can be accessed (www.naceweb.org/principles/). Separating the "wheat from the chaff" regarding Web-based career information and employment sites is a daunting task for the distance learner without immediate professional support at hand. Institutions that enroll distance learners should develop creative, technologically based, support systems to aid distance learners as they sort through the issues involved.

Online Mentoring and Life Coaching

Zachary (2000) provides an informative article about online mentoring relationships that can help inform the campus debate regarding such services (www.dlrn.org/library/dl/mentoring.html).She outlines the challenges in establishing and maintaining such relationships for both the mentor and the mentee. Establishing the expectations and the limitations of such a relationship by each party is the key to success in such online connections. Training for faculty and staff entering formal distance mentoring relationships can help mentors understand the phases of the relationship and how and when to make referrals to other sources of help. Faculty and others should not enter into such formal relationships without understanding the implications of such a connection.

Also available online are numerous Web sites promising life and career coaching for a fee. Because life and career coaches are not required to have specific educational qualifications, ongoing certification, or licensing to practice in most states, the efficacy of such services is difficult to evaluate. This range of for-profit, online businesses could potentially be either helpful or harmful to a student seeking a connection with a professional helper via technology. The distance learner, isolated from direct access to campus career counseling, may be placed in a particularly vulnerable position. Student affairs must determine what role the profession can and should play in providing direct career development assistance to distance learners, as well as assisting such students in becoming better-informed consumers of such services.

Personal Counseling

A range of services is offered via the Internet related to personal counseling. Ford (2000) describes the counseling offered on the Internet as a continuum of services. At one end of the continuum are virtual self-help pamphlet collections on topics such as alcohol and drug abuse, eating disorders, and depression. The other end of the continuum includes actual interaction with a counselor via e-mail or real-time chats or participation in an online support group. Although many sites indicate that the services provided on the site cannot and should not substitute for face-to-face counseling, is that disclaimer enough? Many Web sites are for-profit ventures and are available to anyone, including students enrolled in distance or on-campus learning. What should be the response of the institution to such sites, and what types of institutional support and referral should be available to distance learners seeking psychological services?

The ethical implications of providing therapy through technology should be taken very seriously. Online, telephone, teleconferencing, and e-mail counseling can be seen as an attractive option to many individuals in distress. Such services provide a quick response, and there is a perceived feeling of anonymity for the individual using the service. However, there are a number of issues that must be addressed. Can a clear and correct diagnosis be accomplished online? Can treatment for severe disorders take place in this medium? Finally, how are issues of potential harm to self or others addressed through *cyber-counseling*? In addition, the security of e-mail or Web sites is suspect, and encouraging individuals to share their most private thoughts and feelings in such a venue is risky (Shapiro and Shulman, 2003).

Because of these concerns, professional associations, including the National Board of Certified Counselors, the American Counseling Association, and the American Psychological Association (APA) have issued statements and have developed standards and guidelines for such services. For example, the statement by the Ethics Committee of APA (www.apa.org) indicates that the ethical standards involved in providing psychological services through technology are no less than what is required in face-to-face relationships. But does the distance learner know this? In addition, because the major generalist professional associations including NASPA and ACPA do not address these issues in their own ethical codes, student affairs professionals may not be aware of their obligations to students in this important area of professional practice.

In addition, technology has also changed how psychological services are provided by colleges and universities. Most college counseling centers have some presence on the Internet and provide basic information about accessing services through that medium. Many counseling centers have on-call therapists who respond to students in distress via the telephone when the center is not open and assess what steps should be taken next. Some psychological services centers have twenty-four-hour help lines staffed by graduate students or trained student paraprofessionals, who listen and make referrals, if needed, when a student calls.

Movement toward providing direct services over the Internet has been slower from college counseling centers as such centers have, at the very least, the same ethical and confidentiality issues as face-to-face interactions. In addition, many feel that institutions also have a special obligation to those who enroll as students. Two different approaches, one by the University of North Carolina at Greensboro and the other by Columbia University, are illustrative of the diverse technological pathways regarding counseling taken by institutions of higher education.

The site at the University of North Carolina at Greensboro was a cyber-counseling site focused on providing information to those who visit it about online counseling. The site, which closed in 2003, focused on best practices in and support information about online counseling. Columbia University, on the other hand, provides an online question-and-answer service focusing on a range of both psychological and personal health problems encountered by college students (www.goaskalice.com). The focus of the Columbia site is to make appropriate referrals, let users know that they are not alone, and provide clear and correct information in responses.

Each institution must make clear policy decisions regarding online counseling resources. First, a determination needs to be made regarding what counseling services and information that the institution will offer over the Internet or through other technologies. The second decision requires the institution to examine how such services are presented to students at a distance and on the home campus. The implications of those decisions are profound and should not be left to technology personnel on the campus, because what *can* be done and what *should* be done might well be two very different things.

Branch Campuses and Off-Campus Centers

Student affairs administration on branch campuses and off-campus centers presents a different set of questions and challenges than administration of student affairs at regional institutions.

Branch Campuses

After World War II, the enrollment in American higher education grew rapidly and resulted in increased diversification of the educational enterprise. The emergence of the multicampus university system occurred in the period between 1945 and 1970, and, concurrently, the public community college system expanded. Astin (1997) indicated that after 1950 most states, by policy, favored the construction of commuter institutions (either branch campuses or freestanding institutions) and community colleges. This policy decision dramatically changed the concept of the collegiate educational experience and paved the way for the use of technology as a higher education instructional tool.

The Pennsylvania State University provides an excellent example of the influence of state policy. A strong central campus is connected to branch campuses geographically scattered across the state. As expectations for access to education grow and change, Penn State is dealing with issues related to what student services, programs, and activities should be provided on those branch campuses and in what manner. The Ohio State University is also dealing with some of the same issues and is answering the question of whether residential facilities should be provided at its branch campuses.

The organizational structure in support of student affairs on branch campuses also brings a number of issues and questions. Should the student affairs component on the branch campus be supervised and report to the central campus vice president or provost of student affairs? If the answer is yes, then what is the relationship between the student affairs senior officer on the branch campus to the chief executive of that campus? Where is the locus of control for clinical supervision of services such as counseling and health care on the branch campus? Should branch campuses have their own organizational structure and reporting relationships duplicating that of the central campus? These questions are not easy nor are there easy answers to them. For example, technology can help with the answer to some of these questions by providing online consultation from main to branch campuses, but political and circumstantial realities will likely shape the structures developed on any multicampus institution.

Off-Campus Centers

Komives and Woodard (2003) urge student affairs professionals to expand all of our practices to include distance learners. In addition, they urge student affairs organizations at four-year institutions to develop partnerships with local agencies and community colleges to support distance learners (p. 651). All too often academic courses have been moved closer to students without any planning for services to support students attending those classes. Both undergraduate and graduate students participate in classes where "the faculty member comes to them." Such programs are often the result of marketing efforts to both attract and retain new students. Currently, there is great competition between public and private and proprietary institutions for these new students. Woodard, Love, and Komives (2000) remind us, "For many years, higher education, except for the community colleges and proprietary schools, operated without much influence from the marketplace" (p. 10). That state of affairs has certainly changed and the competition is bound to increase in the future.

Whether the off-campus location has developed as a structural location owned by the main campus or is merely rental space in commercial or governmental property, students are enrolling in record numbers and taking classes in these off-campus locations. Student affairs professionals, for the most part, have not been involved in the design and development of such instructional locations and development of any services for those who attend at these locations are notably sparse. Komives and Woodard (2003) challenge us to "Reach out to all units expanding the scope of their programs to assess student needs and aid in designing programs and interventions" (p. 651). That is good advice, for to do less means that the student affairs profession is not serving a substantial part of the student population of the institution.

Cooperative Education, Internships, and Study Abroad

Many students participate in academic programs that require them to be off campus. Cooperative education, internships, and study abroad are all examples of students engaging in a learning experience far from their home campus. The absence from the home campus can range from ten to fifteen hours a week while carrying a full-time course load (internships), to a summer or a semester while participating in a cooperative education program in a partner company or government agency, or a full semester or calendar year studying at another institution located in another country. Each of these educational opportunities brings both great opportunities and great challenges to student participants. The question for the student affairs profession is what responsibility, if any, does student affairs hold for students engaged in such learning opportunities?

Cooperative Education

Simply defined, cooperative education programs permit the student to alternate periods of study with periods of employment related to the individual interests and goals of the students: academic, career, or personal. Northeastern University, in Boston Massachusetts, has a long-established cooperative education program (co-op) with extraordinarily high participation rates by undergraduate students because cooperative education opportunities are offered in all academic major fields provided by the institution. The typical student participates in three co-ops, each lasting approximately six months for a total of eighteen months of paid work experience prior to graduation. The Northeastern cooperative education experience is supported through an extensive career services program that can be used while the student is on co-op and back on the home campus. In addition, a faculty co-op coordinator is available to directly assist the student both during the actual work experience and in the integration back to the campus. The Northeastern program is very extensive and embedded into the core of the institution, but co-op education programs have also been successfully developed in conjunction with many academic programs in many colleges and universities across the country.

The key to a successful cooperative education experience seems to lie in the preparation and orientation of the student prior to the first co-op assignment. Student affairs programs and services have a great deal to offer to the cooperative educational experience of students, yet on many campuses they have not been partners in development of such programs and only appear to get involved when a student encounters some sort of difficulty while participating in co-op or upon the return of the student to campus. Determining what services and information can and should be available for co-op students should be a key function of student affairs. Students enrolled in co-op are students first, despite their temporary assignment in the world of work. The Northeastern University Division of Cooperative Education Web site can provide some helpful information regarding a possible array of services for cooperative education participants (www.coop.neu.edu/general/index.html).

Internships

There has been great growth in internship programs related to academic programs on many college campuses. A wide range of internship opportunities are available in business, industry, government service, and social service agencies. An internship can range from a full-time experience to a part-time assignment while fully engaged in traditional academic study on the campus. Many internship programs are part of the campus career development center, but a decentralized model is in place on many campuses that relies more on the informal contacts of faculty members than on any formal internship coordination.

No matter what the arrangement, a central question that must be answered is where the locus of responsibility rests when students encounter difficulty in their internship experience. For example, where should students turn if they have experienced racial discrimination, stalking, or sexual harassment while participating in an internship? What preparation and information should be provided to students anticipating participation in internships? Who holds responsibility for checking the appropriateness of the internship site? Because such experiences are often for academic credit, the supervision of many internship programs has traditionally been in the academic schools or departments or programs. However, student affairs needs to examine what role, if any, they should play in resolving problems and what assistance they can provide to this important educational experience for students.

Study Abroad

Trends regarding the participation of American students in study abroad and international exchange and work programs are encouraging, but the growth in study abroad is not what some anticipated a decade ago (Davis, 1997). Only about 1 percent of students in the United States presently study abroad (Christie and Ragans, 1999), and terrorism has caused even more concern on the part of parents and students regarding this educational opportunity. However, the advent of technology and advances in transportation, as well as a globally linked economy, have made study abroad an educational option that will be considered by more and more students in the years ahead.

Study abroad programs on most campuses are directly linked to the academic programs of the institution. Historically, student affairs has not taken a central role in the development and implementation of study abroad programs. In fact, some campuses do not have a study abroad office and instead rely on other agencies or consortiums to provide access to educational opportunities abroad for their students. Whether the institution is directly linked to study abroad programs or participates in a consortium, students studying abroad face the same developmental challenges as their U.S. based counterparts. The question the student affairs professional must ask is what support systems are in place for students studying abroad? Do they have access to appropriate health care? What information is received regarding how to handle emergencies? What training is provided to the on-site coordinators of the study abroad program? How is the home campus informed of any problems and who is the contact person for such situations? What should happen when students experience psychological crises, a medical emergency, or a sexual assault when they are studying in another country? These are but a few of the questions that must be answered and confronted if a study abroad program is to be successful.

One alternative, for example, is provided by the Institute for International Education of Students (IES). IES has developed a system whereby a consulting psychologist with campus experience helps develop the training of on-site staff members dealing with American students. This psychologist is also available to consult with the on-site staff member who is dealing with a difficult issue or concern involving a student. Another approach involves hiring student affairs staff to live and work at large study abroad sites serving as a representative of the sponsoring institution. Other models are certainly possible, but as student affairs professionals know, the out-of-class experience of students has a direct and important influence on their formal educational experience.

There are a number of sources of help for student affairs professionals interested in study abroad and other aspects of international education. These include the National Association of International Educators (NAFSA), a group that was formerly known as the National Association of Foreign Student Advisers (www.nafsa.org/). Studyabroad.com also provides links to a number of programs and work opportunities for students and has helpful advice for a student who is considering study abroad. At the very least, Latham and Dalton (1999) urge student affairs professionals to "become familiar with the international programs in which your institution participates" (p. 90). They urge student affairs administrators to become engaged in international education to ensure that students are being exposed to issues and concerns beyond national borders, for that is the world in which they will live.

Suggestions for Action

In an era of more restricted resources, adding new responsibilities and services is the last thing on the mind of most student affairs professionals. The agendas of student affairs professionals are already daunting on many campuses. Yet the expansion of non-traditional educational settings is happening and will continue to happen with or without the involvement of student affairs. The issues to be dealt with include but are not limited to the following.

1. *Determine oversight responsibility for the function.* Almost all of the non-traditional learning settings discussed in this chapter are not administratively affiliated with most student affairs organizations. Planning and design of such programs is usually vested in academic affairs. Student affairs professionals will need to become more assertive as programs are designed and implemented. Issues related to student health and welfare, in all of these settings, will need to be addressed in a more comprehensive way by institutions, and expectations for a seamless institutional experience for all students will continue to rise.

2. *Understand student expectations.* There is no clarity about what services can and should be offered to students enrolled in distance learning programs. The question of what such students both expect and need from the institution and student affairs will need to be answered on each campus engaged in distance learning experiences described in this chapter. Access to core administrative functions including academic advising appears to be important to such learners, but what expectations do they hold for access to other services?

3. *Encourage evaluation of experiences by student participants.* Sound evaluation of all aspects of distance learning programs needs to occur. Questions regarding the expectations of students participating in such programs, the effectiveness of the programs in meeting those expectations, and the cost-effectiveness of these modes of instruction need to be answered. In addition, a number of ethical questions must be addressed by institutions involved in distance learning. Basic questions regarding access to core administrative functions and other services need to be answered, including the following: What services are possible for distance learners to receive? What should not be provided because of legal or ethical issues regarding counseling and health care? These are not easy questions,

but a sound evaluation program focusing on all aspects of the learning environment may help inform the decision.

4. *Do not abrogate program control to technologists.* Just because it is possible to do something does not mean that it should be done. All too often, student affairs professionals and other academicians have abrogated their responsibilities to technological staff regarding what should be done using the Internet or other innovations. The range and scope of distance learning opportunities should be developed by those with instructional and service experience. For example, until the ethical issues are resolved regarding provision of online counseling services to students, is it wise to do so even if such services can technically be provided through system sophistication? Build partnerships with academic colleagues to provide support programs for distance learners under the supervision of trained professionals in student affairs. The Western Cooperative for Education Telecommunications founded by the Western Interstate Commission for Higher Education has very helpful guidance for creating online student services (Shea and Armitage, 2002).

5. *Determine whether students are receiving fair value for tuition dollars.* Students taking courses in remote locations or via technology often pay the same tuition rates as on-campus students. Some institutions exempt such learners from campus-based fees, but distance learners usually are paying the same tuition as students enrolled in classes on campus. What general support, in addition to the course they are enrolled in, are they receiving for their tuition dollars? When distance learners are not exempt from campus-based fees, what services do they get for their investment? Even though duplication of campus-based services is certainly not possible in every setting, innovative approaches to providing such services via contracts or other means should be explored.

6. *Define service boundaries.* Student affairs has often defined its mission and scope in relationship to students on the physical campus. As technology advances, transportation improves, and world conditions become more peaceful, the lure of non-traditional educational

venues will grow for all students. In order to influence both policy and practice as such alternatives are posed, student affairs must expand its view of whom it serves, under what conditions, and by what means.

The cost of expanding services in any venue is always a legitimate question for student affairs. Is it possible to financially support student services programs for students in non-traditional settings? And if the answer is no, what alternatives should be explored? For example, arrangements might be made to provide initial counseling evaluations for distance learners at community-based mental health centers or the local community college. Creativity will become even more essential as student affairs explores new opportunities for assistance to students.

7. *Define the educational obligations of student affairs.* Technological advances brought both problems and opportunities to society and to higher education. Lots of information is available on the Internet, and some of it is not true, is misleading, or can bring harm to others. Students study in a variety of settings. Student affairs practitioners and others in the academy will need to define the educational obligations they hold for students in a range of educational settings, including the Internet. The volume Documenting Effective Educational Practices (DEEP) (Kuh, Kinzie, Schuh, Whitt, and Associates, 2005) can be extraordinarily helpful in this regard.

8. *Understand the legal issues.* There are a number of legal issues associated with providing educational opportunities either through non-traditional means or in non-traditional settings. Institutions need to be very clear about what they can and cannot promise to students learning in such settings. All written materials and training activities for staff and staff supervision for those working in non-traditional educational settings should include a focus on clarifying policies and procedures for all parties including students. The legal implications of student services in non-traditional settings are many and should be fully explored.

9. *Clarify service limits.* There are limits on what services can be provided and what problems can be avoided in non-traditional

educational settings. As policy and practice in student affairs develop in the arena of non-traditional educational settings, the profession must be clear about what it cannot control and what limits there are on services. To illustrate, it is easy for any student to access the Internet and to receive advice or information that may put them at risk. Many student affairs professionals would like to protect students from such information or advice, but that is impossible. Information, alternatives, questions, and advice should be provided, but ultimately students are responsible for their own lives (National Association of Student Personnel Administrators, 1989).

10. *Review organizational structures.* When dealing with multiple campuses, off-site learning centers, and technology, a number of organizational issues come to mind. Who should be involved in making decisions about services in such settings and where should the locus of control be placed? Although it is clear that academic matters are the responsibility of the faculty and academic affairs, on most main campuses responsibility for student life issues at branch campuses, study abroad, cooperative education programs, and technologically linked ventures are less clear. These vague organizational issues must be addressed. Non-traditional educational settings are likely to grow in the years ahead. Student affairs cannot and should not abrogate their responsibilities to students in those settings.

11. *Become informed about campus activity in non-traditional settings.* For far too long, student affairs professionals have been absent from the processes involved in developing and implementing educational opportunities for students in non-traditional educational settings. The leadership in student affairs must get actively involved in determining what opportunities and support are available to students as they participate in the wide range of learning opportunities available to them. Identify what activities are occurring and find out if any problems have occurred in the past. Get involved in the orientation sessions for students studying abroad and clarify responsibilities between student affairs and study abroad staff.

Summary

As higher education grows and evolves and new methods of instruction and learning are introduced, student affairs must be involved in the process. By thinking outside the traditional realms of service delivery and policy development and always asking if there is a better way to serve students both on- and off-campus, student affairs can make a significant contribution to the learning experiences within their institutions.

In addition, professionals should encourage NASPA, ACPA, and other professional organizations to address the ethical and organizational issues regarding student affairs' participation in distance learning programs. Requests should also be made to the Council for the Advancement of Standards (CAS) to include non-traditional educational environments as CAS develops standards for the specialty areas in student affairs.

Student affairs can and should provide leadership in discussions regarding policies and programs influencing the learning experiences of students in non-traditional settings. Failure to do so means that, as a profession, they are not serving an important segment of the enrolled student population.

7

What Is the Role of Student Affairs in Assessment?

Educators have always wanted to know if their students are actually learning what they have been taught. For several decades in American higher education, faculty, administrators, and educational researchers have been seeking answers to questions about student needs, student attitudes and values, student learning outcomes, student satisfaction, and many other topics. This curiosity about "how we are doing" has become a major force in education at all levels and is now widely known as *assessment*. Student affairs leaders have been quite active in assessment activities in recent years, and this issue is now very important to the successful practice of student affairs. In this chapter, the beginnings of assessment activities in student affairs are discussed; major assessment issues in higher education are presented; various problems and functions of assessment in student affairs are considered; and examples of successful assessment programs are offered. The chapter concludes with suggestions for action for student affairs leaders concerned with assessment.

Some Background on Assessment in Student Affairs

Assessment has been a topic of concern for student affairs professionals going back to the days when the profession was just getting started.

Efforts of Early Deans

Writing in 1910, when the student affairs profession was in its infancy, Marion Talbot, one of the legendary early deans of women, argued that "a study of the motives and influences which lead students in choosing their courses where the elective system prevails will bring into clearer light the present needs on the academic side" (p. 176). It was not called assessment at that time, but Talbot recognized the need to gather data about students so that decisions about their learning could be improved.

In 1929, Esther Lloyd-Jones devoted an entire chapter to "Personnel Research as an Aid in College Administration" in her pioneering book on student affairs. In commenting on the need for systematic studies of students, her office conducted a general survey of the "intellectual life and activities of the campus" at Northwestern University. She formed committees of students, faculty, and staff to inquire about student experiences in a wide range of activities. Lloyd-Jones was as usual ahead of her times, not only in using formal studies to improve student affairs work but also in finding ways to use assessment as an effective way of involving faculty in student affairs.

The Student Personnel Point of View and Influential Authors

In 1937, when the most prominent student affairs leaders of the day met in Washington, D.C., for the purpose of defining the essential characteristics of successful campus student affairs programs, the result was the most influential document ever published in the field: *The Student Personnel Point of View*. Number twenty-three in the authors' list of essential functions was "carrying on studies designed to evaluate and improve these functions and services" (American Council on Education, 1937). While the field was still struggling to find its identity and gain its acceptance in higher education, these leaders understood that a commitment to assessment was critical to future success.

In 1961, Kate Mueller wrote the most influential book on student affairs administration of that time and said this about assessment: "Personnel workers must enumerate their goals and their projects, then investigate their methods and accomplishments. They owe it to themselves the testing and improvement of their own hunches and claims, and to their students and their campus the best approximations of program to goals" (p. 552). She viewed assessment as a professional responsibility for those engaged in student affairs. In this same year, E. G. Williamson, dean of students at the University of Minnesota, argued in his book that "personnel workers should be engaged in constant evaluation of their efforts" (1961, p. 131).

Assessment Not a Priority for Practicing Deans

But even though such leaders urged the importance of assessment activities to the profession, very few student affairs practitioners actually engaged in any research or evaluation. Such activity may have been acknowledged as important, but in the hectic schedules of most student affairs staff, it was most often relegated to the bottom of the priority list. Moreover, student affairs administrators understood that worthwhile assessment activities required research expertise, something many of them did not possess. As a result, for many years, the student affairs field depended almost entirely on studies about students and student learning conducted by educators formally outside the field of student affairs, especially from those in psychology. The work of Theodore Newcomb on student peer groups (1966), Nevitt Sanford on college alumni (1962), Philip Jacob on student values (1957), and Edward Eddy on student character (1959) are examples of such studies during that time.

Lack of Agreement on What to Assess

Even among student affairs professionals who were most interested in assessment activity in student affairs, there was often little agreement about what was most important to study. Simple surveys that provided quick feedback about student satisfaction with a particular program (for example, orientation) often were the norm, and more substantive, longitudinal studies of what students were learning in college were not often pursued. Student affairs administrators, frequently dealing with limited resources, may have wanted to establish an ongoing assessment and evaluation office, but the press of other needs was often so strong that few ever took the initiative to do so. The best assessment programs are usually local in nature (Upcraft, 2003). The University of Minnesota's student affairs program during the period, 1940–1960, was the best institutional example of how assessment can be an integral part of the organization (Wrenn, 1951).

Dependence on Scholars Outside Student Affairs

Until 1965, most student affairs administrators were not very engaged in assessment and were largely dependent on research conducted by psychologists not directly connected to the administration of student affairs. Many of the findings and insights from this research on students were valuable, but there is scant evidence that they had any substantial impact on the actual practice of student affairs.

There were radical changes taking place in American society and in colleges and universities in the 1960s—student enrollment soared, racial and ethnic diversity increased, gender roles changed, the curriculum was in turmoil, and campuses became hot beds of social unrest. Student affairs leaders were under great pressure to deal constructively with these issues, and the best among them recognized that they needed better information about students, their campus experiences, and their learning if they were to succeed in their positions (Sandeen, 2001a). Student affairs assessment efforts began to grow during this period, but they must be viewed as part of a much larger movement—the public's demand for accountability in higher education. Colleges and universities, mainly in response to external pressures, focused on efforts to assess student learning.

The Assessment Movement in American Higher Education

What Is Assessment?

Although assessment has now become a dominant issue in higher education, there has been some confusion about its most appropriate definition. Upcraft and Schuh's definition seems to be the most inclusive: "Assessment is any effort to gather, analyze, and interpret evidence, which describes institutional, divisional, and agency effectiveness" (1996, p. 18). Assessment is not restricted to students and their learning outcomes but may include costs, satisfaction, needs, standards, and benchmarking. It is common to include faculty, administrators, trustees, legislators, alumni, and accrediting agencies.

Higher Education Growth Means More Public Scrutiny

As higher education expanded rapidly and as public expenditures for colleges and universities multiplied after 1965, it was inevitable that greater scrutiny would be given to the issues of quality, productivity, cost-effectiveness, and student learning outcomes. Alexander Astin, a longtime leader in this field, observed that "one of the distinguishing features of American colleges and universities is their fondness for assessment. Practically everybody in the academic community gets assessed these days, and practically everybody assesses somebody else!" (Astin, 1991, p. ix). Even though his work is widely used and respected, Astin himself remains quite skeptical about how much research results and assessments are actually used by faculty and academic leaders and how much of it has proven beneficial in efforts to improve student learning (p. 1). In spite of this, students are assessed in the admissions process and of course in their classes; professors are evaluated by students; professors assess one another in the tenure and promotion process; administrators evaluate one another; and governing boards assess presidential performance. The entire institution is subject to regular assessment by regional and specialized accrediting teams. In response to mandates from state legislators and governors, Gates (2002, p. 115) indicates that "accountability systems have been established to measure the quality of institutions."

Assessment No Longer an Add-On

Assessment in public higher education is no longer simply an "add-on" or something that is peripheral to the institution's overall education program. It is at the center stage of colleges and universities, and it may be the dominant issue in American higher education now, as the forces driving assessment have in effect moved many of the critical decisions institutions make increasingly to external bodies, such as state legislatures and accrediting associations. Assessment is a reality that academic leaders cannot ignore. Peter Ewell (2003) recently observed that in 1990, some academic leaders mistakenly thought that assessment was just another "craze that would go away," and pointed out that the National Center for Public Policy in Higher Education gave all fifty states a grade of incomplete in student learning, while calling for the establishment of a collegiate equivalent of the K–12 learning benchmark, the National Assessment of Educational Progress (p. 4). Some scholars argued that "no development in higher education during these years has created more fundamental change than assessment" (Gaither, Nedwek, and Neal, 1994).

Impact of National Higher Education Reports

During the 1980s, many educators as well as the general public began to recognize the need for assessment in higher education. There was a good deal of unrest regarding the quality of higher education, and this was dramatically expressed in three influential national reports: *Integrity in the College Curriculum* (Association of American Colleges, 1985); *Time for Results: The Governors' Report on Education* (National Governors Association, 1986); and *Involvement in Learning: Realizing the Potential of American Higher Education* (National Institute on Education, 1984). These reports focused attention on the preparation of college graduates and raised the question, "Were students learning and what should they be learning?" (Palomba and Banta, 1999, p. 1). The first national conference on assessment in higher education was held in Columbia, South Carolina, in the fall of 1985, and over seven hundred college and university leaders attended, a clear indication of the growing importance of this issue (Banta, 2002, p. 7). The American College Testing Program developed its Collegiate Assessment of Academic Proficiency exam (ACT), representing the readiness of external agencies to provide "off-the-shelf" types of tests for use in evaluating student learning. The National Educational Goals Panel established the nation's first objectives for collegiate learning, with proposed tests on critical thinking, communication skills, and problem solving (1991).

External Pressures to Assess

Ewell (1999) argues that many colleges and universities are actually doing assessment because somebody told them to, as opposed to really believing in it. He further suggests that some institutions remain content to do assessment in terms of what others demand and are not yet engaged in assessment in the spirit of real academic improvement. The tension between what institutions want to pursue in assessing their own educational programs and what state governments and accrediting bodies require them to do is very likely to continue for some time. Burke and Serban (1998, p. 1) state that "critics charged that public colleges and universities admitted too many underprepared students, graduated too few of those enrolled, permitted too many to take too long to earn degrees, and allowed too many to finish without the knowledge and skills necessary for productive careers." It is not surprising that when facing such harsh criticisms, state after state imposed funding based upon performance and externally determined standards of quality in order to assure the public that the institutions were fulfilling their assigned missions. Hutchings and Marchese (1990, p. 12), in discussing assessment's role in higher education, argue that "as a phenomenon, it is at once powerful, scary in the wrong hands, increasingly a matter of law, and home to the day's most provocative decisions of teaching and learning. The one sure thing is that assessment warrants close attention."

Role of Accrediting Agencies

Regional accrediting associations also have played a significant role in what assessment has become in the past twenty years. Faced with biting criticism from state governments and the Congress (Education Commission of the States, 1994) for focusing too heavily upon mere compliance with standards, all six major accrediting associations have shifted the focus of their evaluation; now institutions are required to present evidence that their students are achieving the educational outcomes described in the mission statements of the institution (Wolff, 1992). The future of the traditional accrediting associations has been threatened by state governments and the Congress, who have asked how institutions can continue to receive accreditation when there is so much public dissatisfaction with the quality of college graduates (Lubinescu, Ratcliff, and Gaffney, 2001). This fractious debate between legislatures and accrediting bodies is by no means settled, and assessment is at the center of this debate. Allen and Bresciani (2003, p. 21) argue that "the assessment movement in higher education—with prodding from accrediting agencies and state governments—is gradually moving us from asking exclusively input based questions (like how many faculty per student; how many books are in the library; or how many courses are taught by graduate students versus senior faculty) to asking outcomes based questions (such as what have the students actually learned)."

Shift from the Single Test to Broader Learning Outcomes

An additional issue in the debate about assessment in higher education is the major change that has taken place from what had been the dominant role of assessment for so long. Messick (1999, p. 3) points out that "for most of the 20th century, the face of higher education assessment has displayed a singular countenance. Admissions testing was its salient feature because student selection was the primary function that assessment served." This has been reinforced, of course, by the public's perception that quality is often driven by the SAT exam, or the "Big Test" (Lemann, 1999). This test often has become the single standard by which we judge others and ourselves. Sedlacek (2004, p. 4) suggests "that if a college has students with high SAT scores, many members of the public assume that the students must be learning something, and that the college must be good." But now, the emphasis is increasingly on assessment for the improvement of instruction and student performance, for the certification of learning and competence, and for the evaluation of program quality.

State Legislatures and Assessment

Questions about higher education from state legislators include "Can we take the word of educators that all is well with the enterprise?" and "Are we getting our money's worth?" (Delco, 1989, p. 4). Such questions have placed academic leaders on the defensive, and the concept of the *academic audit* (Massy, 2003) has been introduced in several states to monitor the quality of educational programs. Recently, in the State University of New York system, a program was introduced to administer an assessment test to undergraduates, covering math, basic communication, critical thinking, information management, and methods used to explore phenomena (Hebel, 2004, p. 20).

National Center for Postsecondary Improvement Project

Among the most significant recent efforts to assess higher education is a project conducted by the National Center for Postsecondary Improvement, the "Report to Stakeholders on the Condition and Effectiveness of Postsecondary Education." The center has issued three reports since 2001, published in *Change* magazine. They have focused on the recent college graduate (2001a), the public (2001b), and the employers (*Change*, 2002). The results, based on surveys, indicated that there is a good deal of support among the public for what higher education is doing, although there are many perceived shortcomings as well. The studies also found a clear link between perceptions of higher education's value and the condition of the economy at the time: so long as students find gainful employment that maintains or improves their socioeconomic status, the students, the public, and the employers seem pleased. However, such findings, although certainly of interest, do not provide much insight into the substance or improvement of student learning, which is the academy's major focus regarding assessment.

The Impact of Rankings

Assessment in higher education has become a very public issue, as demonstrated by the national interest created annually by the *U.S. News & World Report*'s college ranking issue (2004). Many educators continue to criticize these popular rankings (Hossler, 2000), but many institutions use information from these rankings in their recruiting materials and on their Web sites, in obvious attempts to convince prospective students (and their parents) of the college's quality. The popularity of these rankings is an obvious indication that large numbers of the public are concerned about educational quality, or at least, in having their children attend colleges that are considered to be among "the best."

The National Survey of Student Engagement

Perhaps the most encouraging development in recent years to provide colleges, students, and the public with useful information about how students actually participate in various educational practices is the National Survey of Student Engagement (NSSE). This instrument features five benchmarks: level of academic challenge, active and collaborative learning, student interactions with faculty members, enriching educational experiences, and supportive campus environment (Kuh, 2001). The survey has been used by hundreds of colleges and universities, and although its primary benefit is designed to assist institutions to improve their educational programs, the NSSE may become a valuable way for the public to assess the actual characteristics of the learning environment of a campus. Instead of focusing merely on academic reputation or resources, the NSSE provides data about the extent to which students participate in a number of educational practices known to be associated with good learning.

A Raucous Debate

Because of the volatility and high visibility of the assessment issue, the debate has often become raucous during the past few years. Turnbull (1985, p. 23) urged those involved in this debate to remember that "the overriding purpose of gathering data is to provide a basis for improving instruction, rather than keeping score or allocating blame." Peter Ewell, one of the most respected leaders in higher education assessment, argues that "both the current politics and a new operating environment for higher education are forcing an action agenda for colleges and universities that will increasingly have assessment at its center—whether we or they like it or not. The need for quality assurance for the academy's many publics is real and permanent, despite surface fluctuations" (1999, p. 155). Another prominent leader in assessment, Trudy Banta, points out that "there is a palpable tension between the two principle purposes of assessment: demonstrating accountability and improving curricula instruction, and student services" (1993, p. 352). This tension is certain to continue, as higher education leaders are caught between the quantified measures imposed by external evaluators and the insistence of their own faculty to focus on more substantive measures of student learning.

Assessment Now a Powerful Force in Higher Education

As this brief summary has shown, assessment in higher education has become the most powerful force in driving the decisions of colleges and universities. It is not likely to go away. Courts and McInerney (1993, p. xiii) described the situation well: "The American educational system appears to be poised on the edge of a revolution. It may be symbolized by either a guillotine threatening any and all who choose to dispute the sense of imposed assessment mandates, or as a new educational constitution that details the rights and responsibilities of teachers and learners."

Student affairs leaders are now conducting their work within this overall context of assessment in higher education. It is important for them to know its origins, to understand the issues being debated, and most important, to become full participants in their institution's assessment programs. A discussion of the current state of assessment in student affairs is now presented.

Student Affairs and Assessment

Recognizing and accepting that the assessment movement is here to stay, student affairs professionals need to be effective and to rise to the challenge.

The Field Matures After 1965

After 1965, the amount and quality of research within student affairs increased dramatically. Previously dependent mainly upon studies and research conducted by those outside the profession, several investigators from within student affairs produced extremely valuable findings about student learning outcomes, student characteristics, diversity, and other issues. Chickering and Reisser's *Education and Identity* (1993); Astin's *What Matters in College: Four Critical Years Revisited* (1993); Katz's *No Time for Youth: Growth and Constraint in College Students* (1969); Kuh, Schuh, and Whitt's *Involving Colleges: Successful Approaches to Fostering Learning and*

Development Outside the Classroom (1991); and Pascarella and Terenzini's *How College Affects Students* (1991, 2005) are prominent examples of the excellence that now characterizes the field. These books, and other studies by the same authors (for example, Astin, *Achieving Educational Excellence*, 1985), stimulated a significant number of projects by others (for example, American Association for Higher Education, 2004), and this has also been reflected in the improved quality and sophistication of the professional journals in the field.

By 1985, the year when the assessment movement in higher education seemed to "explode" on the scene, many leaders in student affairs were actually ahead of the curve, as they had already been involved with studies about student characteristics, learning outcomes, gender and racial issues, student needs, and student satisfaction. But as will be discussed later in this chapter, in many cases, this early assessment work in student affairs was often conducted without much fanfare, and without significant support or attention from campus faculty and academic administrators. Indeed, even Alexander Astin, the most active researcher in this field during the past three decades, has expressed doubt about the willingness of faculty and academic leaders to use assessment results as a basis for improving student learning (Astin, 1991, p. ix).

Upcraft and Schuh Lead the Way

When Lee Upcraft and John Schuh published their book *Assessment in Student Affairs: A Guide for Practitioners* (1996), it was received with enthusiasm throughout the profession. Their work has stimulated student affairs leaders to initiate assessment programs on their campuses and has led to a large number of state, regional, and national conferences, seminars, and workshops on the topic of student affairs assessment. Recently, they published *Assessment Practice in Student Affairs: An Applications Manual* (2001) that provides further guidance for campus student affairs leaders wanting to implement and improve their assessment practices.

Upcraft (2003, p. 558) suggests that "student affairs is under considerable pressure to demonstrate its importance and worth." With institutional resources declining, the competition for financial support often becomes fierce, and student affairs' programs may be subjected to very careful scrutiny. In some cases, this situation has led student affairs leaders to approach assessment in a defensive mode, feeling as if they need to provide evidence of their worth in order to maintain what they have. This is a reason that Upcraft (2003, p. 560) argues that all assessment is political; that is, it is never done in isolation from other campus issues, whether they are financial, academic, or service related.

Risks and Benefits for Student Affairs in Assessment

There are obvious risks for student affairs leaders in assessment, as results from various studies may reveal some embarrassing weaknesses and shortcomings in various programs. The temptation for student affairs staff may be to avoid certain issues or only to conduct safe studies that will not reflect poorly on their programs or impinge on areas outside student affairs. Integrity in assessment is absolutely necessary to achieve results that can improve the quality of education; student affairs staff deal with critical issues that affect the lives and the educational success of students, so any assessment plan that shies away from conducting and publishing studies that address the most important issues is indefensible. Assessment may be the best way to ensure a strong educational and ethical commitment to quality services and programs in student affairs.

Upcraft and Schuh (1996) argue that assessment programs in student affairs can improve quality; guide strategic planning; analyze cost-effectiveness; justify programs and services; assist in accreditation; and guide decision making, policies, and practices. They have proposed an eight-part assessment model for student affairs, which includes keeping track of who uses services, using national standards to assess learning, assessing comparable institutional programs, and assessing student needs, satisfaction, campus environments and cultures, costs, and outcomes. Their model also urges keeping track of who uses services, programs, and facilities and using national standards of good practices in assessment.

George Kuh, in directing the National Survey of Student Engagement project, has introduced highly useful and credible ways of viewing students' educational experiences on the campus. His approach to assessment focuses on helping institutions understand how students interact with faculty, staff, and other students in a variety of in-class and out-of-class settings. It builds on his and others' earlier work that demonstrated that "the impact of college is most potent when in-class and out-of class experiences are complementary" (Kuh, 1997, p. 71). This valuable information can stimulate study and discussion about ways to improve educational experiences for students on the campus and in the process bring faculty, students, and student affairs staff together in cooperative efforts. Kuh's work may also enable prospective students and the public to learn substantive educational information about the institution's educational program in ways not previously available. Kuh argues that "sooner or later, colleges and universities are either going to demonstrate what their students are learning or some external entity will impose its own approach" (2001, p. 10).

The insights and knowledge that have emerged from the work of Ernest Pascarella (1982), Patrick Terenzini (1997), and Vincent Tinto (1987) have advanced student affairs practice and policy in significant ways during the past twenty years. Their studies have addressed such issues as cognitive learning outcomes, the impact of student group affiliations on development, attitudes about diversity, attrition, and student value development. Their work has also stimulated considerable assessment activity on the campuses.

Alexander Astin's research and publications over the past thirty-five years make him one of the most respected and influential leaders in American higher education. From his Higher Education Research Institute (HERI) at UCLA, the annual survey of entering freshmen (Astin, Dey, and Korn, 1991) has provided hundreds of colleges and universities with very usable data about their students, enabling them to view this over many years and to compare it with other institutions. His work on college impact, value-added education, achieving educational excellence, preventing dropouts, the college environment, and other topics have probably done more to advance the student affairs profession than any other researcher.

Arthur Chickering's work on college student development and the conditions related to student learning (Chickering, 1969) have provided student affairs professionals with workable models for campus programs, policies, and co-curricular activities. His work has been extremely important to the assessment movement in student affairs, and he has provided compelling reasons for student affairs staff to collaborate with faculty to achieve improved learning for students. *Applying the Seven Principles for Good Practice in Undergraduate Education* (Chickering and Gamson, 1991) has become one of the most popular and valuable tools used by colleges and universities in the assessment of their campus learning programs.

These researchers and writers have provided the major foundation and stimulus to the encouraging and valuable assessment activity now occurring in student affairs. Among the most notable in the new generation of researchers leading assessment activities important to student affairs are Schuh (2002), Bresciani (2002), Banta (2002), Ewell (1995), Gardner and Upcraft (1989), Gardner and Van der Veer (1998), Magolda and Porterfield (1993), Erwin (2000), Palomba and Banta (2001), Mentkowski and Associates (2000), and Ratcliff (1995).

Student Affairs Research Positions

Only about forty colleges and universities employ a full-time student affairs researcher (Malaney, 1999). As a result, much of the assessment work in student affairs is done by those with other administrative responsibilities, by faculty members affiliated with the student affairs division, or by some collaborative arrangement with the office of institutional research. As indicated by Pickering and Hanson (2000, p. 79), "Too often, student affairs assessment efforts and institutional research functions exist in different worlds, even within the same campus." Edgerton (1987, p. 100) argues that "in the early days, institutional research offices evaluated curricula, assessed student achievement, predicted student success, compared different teaching methods, and studied student attitudes and satisfaction." In recent years, these institutional research offices have often been directed to produce reports on student flow, costs per credit hour, teaching loads, and faculty salaries. Responding mainly to external requirements, many of these offices are not as engaged in investigations of student learning as they once were.

Activity in student affairs assessment has been given additional encouragement and support in *The Student Learning Imperative* (Schroeder and Associates, 1996); in *Good Practice in Student Affairs* (Blimling and Whitt, 1999); in the *Standards and Guidelines for Student Services Development Programs* (CAS, 2003); and in the *Learning Reconsidered* (National Association of Student Personnel Administrators, American College Personnel Association, 2004) documents. All of these publications give strong emphasis to the critical role of assessment in student affairs. They urge student affairs professionals to work with faculty to define in explicit terms the student learning outcomes that their institutions aspire to provide. At the same time, they urge student affairs to be creative about using multiple approaches to assessment of student learning. Schilling and Schilling (1998, p. 250) argue that assessment should not just focus on single measures of student learning but should also include inventories, Web surveys, interviews, presentations, portfolios, student journals, focus groups, case studies, co-curricular transcripts, employer and alumni surveys, and capstone experiences. The Harvard Assessment Seminars provide a good illustration of the potential value of interviewing students about their educational experiences. One interviewed student reported, "What a wonderful opportunity you have given me to reflect on my experiences—the only time in four years I have really been asked to do so!" (Light, 2000, p. 20).

Encouraging Progress in Student Affairs Assessment

The quality and quantity of assessment activity in student affairs is at an all-time high. There is a genuine commitment on behalf of student affairs leaders to make assessment a core component of their programs, policies, and services and to use data gathered from local and national sources to improve the quality of student learning. The assessment movement is one of the most encouraging developments in the student affairs profession in recent years, and it is resulting in improved understanding of students and better policies and programs in student learning.

Despite the impressive advances made in student affairs assessment in recent years, there are some important issues that the profession should consider. These are discussed in the final section of this chapter, and some suggestions for improving practice are also made.

Some Current Shortcomings

Student affairs professionals have many reasons to feel pride in what they have accomplished in the area of assessment in recent years. It represents one of the most positive contributions to the advancement of the profession in its history. Yet there are some shortcomings in how student affairs divisions are conducting their assessment efforts that need to be addressed.

- *Acting Alone.* In their zeal to improve their programs and services, student affairs professionals involved in assessment have too often acted alone. Frequently conducting studies and surveys in areas for which they have administrative responsibility, they may have too much at stake to be completely unbiased in their observations. Moreover, they have sometimes become isolated from the core academic programs of their own campuses. Some of this separation from academic program assessment may be understandable, as very little actual assessment related to student academic outcomes may be taking place on their campuses; in the absence of such activity, student affairs professionals may have grown impatient and may have simply proceeded on their own.

• *Isolation from Campus Institutional Assessment Efforts.* Other student affairs professionals may have felt distant from their institutional research offices, which often have been assigned to do little more than massage financial data for external agencies, rather than addressing substantive assessment issues. This can be very frustrating and often leads to an uncoordinated approach to assessment on the campus.

Most student affairs professionals conducting assessment studies on their campuses are more than happy to share their results (and suggestions) with those who might listen, but too often, they have had difficulty attracting audiences that extend beyond their own division. The professional journals in student affairs have done an excellent job of encouraging and publishing important assessment efforts of professionals in the field; unfortunately, these journals are not widely read outside the student affairs profession, which contributes to the isolation felt by leaders in this field.

• *Narrow Issues and Personal Agendas.* Sometimes local assessment efforts are conducted on issues so specific that they may seem trivial to others outside the field. Worse, some local assessment efforts in student affairs may be poorly disguised efforts to advance a particular agenda on the campus or to gain support for a proposed policy change. When this happens, it is understandable that some campus leaders outside student affairs may become skeptical about such practices and discredit other, very useful efforts.

• *Comfort in Their Own Sphere.* It can become comfortable for some student affairs professionals to pursue their own assessment activities without others paying much attention to what they are doing; they may gain some attention from their professional colleagues engaged in related activities on other campuses, but their efforts may have little or no impact on programs or policies on their own campus. The best assessment programs are those clearly connected to academic and co-curricular programs and policy; findings from various studies need to be shared widely if they are to improve student learning.

• *Lack of Coordination in Assessment.* The lack of coordination within student affairs divisions regarding assessment efforts can seriously reduce any potential impact student affairs might have on campus-wide programs. At a large institution, for example, it may be commendable that assessment activities are being conducted in several of the large student affairs departments; however, if each office is essentially operating on its own in this regard, and no coordination or clear focus is given to these efforts, then the impact on the campus will likely be minimal. It is the responsibility of the senior student affairs officer to ensure effective coordination of such efforts.

• *Disconnect from Core Undergraduate Academic Programs.* A serious current shortcoming for student affairs professionals involved in assessment is their distance from the core undergraduate academic programs of the campus. This is especially the case regarding general education programs. If most (if not all) of the assessment activities in student affairs have been apart from the core academic program of the campus, it is unlikely that student affairs leaders will be asked to assume any significant role in institution-wide assessment programs, especially because institutional assessment now focuses so often on criteria defined by external bodies. This may not be the preferred climate student affairs professionals would choose to engage in assessment activities, but it is now the reality.

• *Senior Student Affairs Officers and Assessment.* Finally, senior student affairs officers have at times not been as forceful in their leadership regarding assessment programs as they should be. They are squeezed from many sides in their positions and rarely have adequate resources to address all of the issues and problems needing attention; nonetheless, some of them have been too passive regarding their own role in assessment. They may have simply assigned this function to someone or may have allowed a variety of disconnected assessment activities to take place within their own divisions. Some of them have not been persuasive contributors to campus-wide assessment efforts, due to their lack of expertise, time constraints, or the press of other duties.

Suggestions for Action

The following suggestions are offered for consideration by the profession.

1. *Strong leadership by senior student affairs officers is the most important change that could improve student affairs' role in assessment.* The senior student affairs officer needs to be very knowledgeable about assessment and, equally as important, a persuasive advocate for the role of student affairs in campus-wide assessment efforts. If the student affairs division is to become a full, contributing participant in the institution's assessment program, it is highly unlikely that this will occur without leadership from the senior student affairs officer. It is the responsibility of the senior student affairs officer to acquire the resources for assessment activities, to establish assessment as a priority, and to ensure that assessment activities are well coordinated within the division. The senior student affairs officer's role is to "tell the story" in a convincing manner to a variety of constituencies, and assessment should be at the heart of the story.

2. *Those directly engaged in student affairs assessment activities should broaden the focus of their interests by working cooperatively with faculty on core academic programs on their campuses.* Student affairs professionals have substantive contributions to make to such efforts and indeed can play a leading role in initiating discussions with faculty colleagues that may lead to improvements in student learning. The undergraduate general education program is often a useful focus for such efforts, as it is usually most clearly related to the stated academic purposes of the institution. Harvard has just published what its faculty deem to be the essential components of its new general

education program (Bartlett, 2004, p. A14). When similar efforts are initiated on other campuses, student affairs professionals should be contributing members of groups assigned to develop such academic programs. This will require student affairs professionals to become more knowledgeable about the content of what undergraduates are actually studying in the classroom and to expand their own views about student learning.

3. *Senior student affairs officers frequently report directly to the president, and this may enable them to have access to institutional resources and to influence major policies and programs.* However, in some cases, this organizational arrangement has resulted in isolation from the academic program of the campus, and occasionally, it has placed the student affairs division in direct competition with academic affairs. Such separate and competing arrangements may no longer be conducive to improving the overall educational programs of the campus (see Chapter Two). If the provost's office controls most of the resources on the campus, and student affairs is viewed as a separate entity, unrelated to core academic programs, then it will be very difficult for student affairs to assume a significant role in campus-wide assessment programs. Collaboration and cooperation are extremely important, but if organizational arrangements become barriers, then other options need to be explored. Previous organizational assumptions about the role of student affairs on the campus may need to be reconsidered, as now, the strong emphasis upon assessment and student learning may be reason for institutions to combine student affairs and academic affairs into one coordinated unit.

4. *Leaders in the student affairs assessment movement should urge collaboration between student affairs professional associations and generalist higher education associations such as the American Council on Education, the National Association of State Universities and Land-Grant Colleges, the National Association of Independent Colleges and Universities, and the American Association for Higher Education.*

The student affairs journals should broaden their approach to assessment, encouraging and publishing studies that focus on core academic programs on the campus, not just local assessment surveys of little interest to those outside student affairs. Senior student affairs officers and leaders in the student affairs assessment movement should insist on the highest professional standards in assessment studies, ensuring the integrity of results. Those who might use assessment to further their own political agendas on the campus will seriously damage the credibility of studies designed to improve the quality of education for students. Senior student affairs officers, working closely with provosts and academic deans, should provide the leadership on these matters.

5. *Assessment in higher education has become such a highly visible and volatile issue that it cannot be ignored by student affairs professionals, even when they find it distasteful or when its priorities are driven by external bodies who are not as committed as they are to diverse and substantive approaches to student learning.* The governance of public colleges and universities is increasingly driven by external forces, and student affairs professionals will not serve any constructive purpose by opting out of the process, no matter how politically unattractive it may appear to be. It may be more pleasant to remain apart from the fickle and increasingly precarious world of institutional assessment, but this is where student affairs professionals need to be. They will not be able to have a major impact on the improvement of student learning if they are not part of the main event.

6. *The excellent assessment initiatives now being conducted by student affairs professionals are commendable, are contributing to the improvement of programs and services on many campuses, and should be continued and enhanced.* But with assessment now as the central driving force in higher education, it has become an institution-wide issue, and student affairs must demonstrate more effective campus leadership to ensure that it is a full participant in improving the quality of education for students.

Summary

Assessment is now the most powerful movement in American higher education. It is not a passing fad, but a reality, and it will continue to have a major impact on how colleges and universities are funded, how they teach, and what students learn. Student affairs professionals have proven themselves very capable of being active participants in this movement, and despite the many challenges they face in assessment, they are now in the best position they have ever been to become important contributors to understanding and assessing the ways students learn.

8

Who Has Responsibility for the Lives of Students?

Determining who has responsibility for the lives of students is a vexing question for many student affairs administrators. Many believe that the concept of *in loco parentis* is settled, but that simply is not true. Changing laws, attitudes, demographics, and relationships all contribute to the complexity of the answer to the question of who has responsibility for the lives and welfare of students. A number of issues are part of the daily lives of student affairs administrators: Should students be responsible for their own lives and decisions? Should students be responsible when they might harm self or others? Does the institution carry some responsibility for the lives and welfare of all students? Are institutions obligated to provide a full range of services for all students throughout their college career? Should parents, family members, the state, or the local community assume part of the cost and part of the responsibility for services for students who need them? All of these questions and many more are facing higher education and student affairs and are not likely to diminish in the years ahead.

The old adage "you cannot be all things to all people" is central to the debate about where responsibility rests for the lives of students. Implicit in that saying is an admonishment to institutions and individuals to set limits; make decisions about how to invest time, energy, and resources; and affirm the principles that support higher education and student affairs. But on the whole, student affairs has not met that challenge. The history and tradition of student affairs contributes to the ambiguity many student affairs professionals are feeling. For example, student affairs units are often the locus of the campus response to new populations or underserved groups. Most of these new responses are added to an already full agenda of programs and services. It is a trend that cannot continue. The available human and fiscal resources are diminishing for the higher education enterprise at the same time that demands for services are increasing. A critical examination of the institutional responsibilities for and to students must occur if the student affairs profession is going to be successful in the future. Such an examination of the issues involved must include both setting priorities for services and identifying realistic limitations of what the institution can and cannot do. The process of developing priorities and boundaries must be both initiated and led by student affairs professionals. Failure to do so will result in further fragmentation of efforts, as limited resources are allocated to an ever-expanding base of needs within the student community. Answering the question of who has responsibility for the lives of students and what are the realistic limitations on those responsibilities is critical to the profession of student affairs and institutions of higher education.

This chapter will identify the primary forces of change that currently influence the professional practice of student affairs, including what services should be provided to students, and it will define the perceived institutional responsibilities to students. Critical questions that must be answered by the profession and higher education will be presented. The barriers that interfere with a rational discussion of what student affairs can and cannot accomplish within the present and future context of American higher education will be identified. The chapter will conclude with suggestions for the profession as the debate goes forth regarding who has responsibility for the lives of students. Resolving this philosophical issue is an important and critical future challenge that must be resolved by the profession of student affairs and institutions of higher education.

Forces of Change

When considered collectively, the number and complexity of the forces of change influencing higher education and student affairs are startling. Major forces of change include changed student characteristics; expanded expectations of parents, students, and others for the higher education experience; a sharply redefined legal environment for higher education; and a changed financial support structure for institutions of higher education. These four major forces of change profoundly shape the debate regarding the locus of responsibility for the lives of students.

Changing Students

Anyone working in student affairs is aware of the far-reaching changes in the characteristics of enrolled students in American higher education. El-Khawas (2003) identified both background and situational factors that contribute to a changed student population in American higher education.

Background Factors

Many background factors of students are observable, including changes in enrollment reflecting more women than men at all educational levels, more non-traditionally aged students, and more racially diverse students. Upcraft and Stephens (2000) state that differences within minority groups may be as great as differences among the aforementioned groups, and they caution student affairs professionals to not reach conclusions based on gross categorizations of race and ethnicity. But racial and cultural diversity must be recognized and understood, for it is a fact of life at most colleges and universities.

Some characteristics, however, may be less apparent, including ethnicity, religion, socioeconomic status, sexual identity, disability, and international student status. All of these background factors directly influence the range and scope of programs, services, and activities provided by student affairs. Background factors also help shape the needs, wants, and desires of enrolled students. To illustrate, students with children have pushed for institutionally supported child-care programs. Students with both visible and invisible disabilities have expectations for support programs that have been shaped, in part, by their K–12 educational experiences. And students from underrepresented populations have demanded changes in institutional policies, programs, and support to help ensure their success in the collegiate environment.

Situational Factors

The situational factors described by El-Khawas (2003) are more opaque and difficult to recognize and analyze. Situational factors include characteristics such as full- or part-time enrollment, studying in whole or in part online, dropping out for personal reasons, financing college expenses, or enrolling only to meet a very specific, limited educational objective, not to obtain a degree.

Woven into both these invisible and visible changes in students are those issues that relate to the question regarding who is responsible for the lives of students. These issues include increases in the number of students enrolled with long-term psychological issues, both visible and invisible disabilities, and the evolving social climate with regard to alcohol use and abuse. Each of these concerns has a direct influence on the question of who holds responsibility for the lives of students.

Psychological Issues

The number of students seen by college and university counseling centers with severe and urgent problems has dramatically increased in the last decade (Gallagher and Zhang, 2003; Benton and others, 2003). The demand for psychological service has grown at the same time that competition for resources within higher education has become more intense. Questions regarding the role of the institution in providing psychological services have been raised on many campuses, including but not limited to the following: What types of psychological services should be provided for students? What limits (if any) should be set for such services? And is the investment in prevention activities by psychological staff cost-effective for the institution?

Regardless of the answers to these questions, students with long-term psychological issues have the potential to cause disruption and distress within the educational community. Delworth (1989) developed a model that is useful to student affairs practitioners when dealing with such students. She categorized students who cause concerns in the educational community into two categories: *disturbing students* and *disturbed students*.

Disturbing students engage in behavior that is either impulsive and immature or controlling and manipulative (Ragle and Justice, 1989). Disturbing students should be confronted when their behavior is not appropriate and also should be held accountable through clear and unambiguous policies and processes within the student discipline system. Ragle and Justice state that "students referred to the judicial system are often on the edge—the edge of the community, in that they have violated the community's norms—and yet at the same time they are potentially on the cutting edge of their own personal development" (p. 29). A well-developed and consistent judicial system can assist students in understanding the consequences of their disturbing behavior whether it involves lying, cheating, stealing, antisocial activities, vandalism, or substance abuse.

Disturbed students can demonstrate either inward focus (depression and withdrawal) or outward focus (anger and lashing out) (Delworth, 1989). Disturbed students hold the potential to bring harm to themselves or to others. These students can engage in a wide variety of behaviors. Sometimes they are withdrawn, sometimes rigid, and sometimes angry. Such students "not only lack a sense of how to establish positive interpersonal relationships, but they also have no interest in doing so" (Delworth, p. 7). Whatever the behaviors, disturbing students require direct intervention by trained psychological staff.

The most difficult situations for student affairs professionals are those involving students who are both disturbed *and* disturbing. Delworth (1989) indicates that these students are most likely to cause the educational environment to be in turmoil and also consume inordinate amounts of time, energy, and focus of the student affairs staff members who must deal with them. Dealing with disturbed and disturbing students in an effective manner requires communication between professionals providing psychological care and those who carry responsibility for enforcing institutional standards. Hollingsworth and Dunkle (2005) define two separate and unambiguous tracks for dealing with such students. One track focuses on the mental health of the student and one focuses on the behavior of that same student. Both tracks can move forward at the same time to bring resolution to the problem. Under such an approach, both the psychological staff and the student affairs administrators must establish clear roles and responsibilities in order to successfully develop solutions that are in the best interests of the student and the institution. Sandeen (1989) reminds us that "priorities for student affairs programs are not determined solely on the basis of economy" (p. 60). He admonishes the student affairs profession to remember that "an institution that decides it cannot afford the resources required to address the problems of the disturbed and disturbing student may discover that the costs of ignoring them are too great" (p. 61).

Disabilities

Since 1973, Section 504 of the Vocational Rehabilitation Act (U.S. Code Vol. 29, secs. 791–794) has prohibited discrimination on the basis of handicap in educational programs receiving federal financial assistance, if the student is otherwise qualified. The Americans with Disabilities Act (ADA) (U.S. Code, Vol. 42. secs. 12101 et. seq.) applies to all employers with twenty-five or more employees, including institutions of higher education. In combination, these statutes have created enormous challenges for student higher education.

Making facilities and programs physically accessible to all h. been expensive and is a continued effort on most campuses. These statutes have opened the doors of higher education to many, including students who are hearing and sight impaired, have mobility challenges, or have diagnosed learning disabilities. Although such accommodations are labor-intensive and costly, such efforts have been accepted and supported at most institutions.

The intersection between the legal requirements posed by these statutes and dealing with students exhibiting severe psychological disabilities, on the other hand, poses very complex issues for student affairs professionals. Those issues are central to the debate about who has responsibility for the lives of students. Gothin (2003) cautions student affairs administrators to not fall into the trap of requiring counseling as part of the discipline process for students. She states, in part, that "when the friendly referral to existing or outside services becomes a mandate to seek counseling as a medical treatment, the institution takes upon itself the burden of policing medical treatment that is beyond its scope" (p. 6). She reminds student affairs administrators to focus on behavior rather than on the psychological status of the student, saying in part, that "it is not reasonable for a student to request an accommodation that allows him to continue to misbehave or merely 'accepts' as part of his illness, his outbursts in class, his refusal to comply with reasonable requests or his violent behavior" (p. 4). Defining reasonable accommodations for students with recognized psychological disabilities requires both understanding of the disability involved *and* understanding of the educational standards and requirements of the institution.

It is clear that dealing with the range and scope of psychological disabilities and setting the parameters of response to requests for accommodations will be among the greatest challenges facing the leadership in student affairs for the decades ahead. Determining what is a reasonable request and what the limitations are regarding what an institution can and should do to accommodate students with psychological disabilities will be a matter of debate for some time into the future.

Alcohol Use and Abuse

The consequences of the abuse of alcohol and other drugs are significant for the individual student involved, for family and friends, and for the campus community. The national statistics regarding high-risk college drinking consequences are very powerful. To illustrate, the Task Force of the National Advisory Council on Alcohol Abuse and Alcoholism (2002) cited the following statistics regarding alcohol abuse: 1,400 deaths of traditionally aged college students each year, 500,000 injuries related to alcohol use each year, 600,000 cases of assault involving alcohol, 400,000 self-reported incidents involving unsafe sex and alcohol use, 25 percent of students reporting academic problems related to alcohol abuse, and 2.1 million incidents of drunk driving involving students eighteen to twenty-four years of age. Yet the abuse and misuse of alcohol continue, fueled in part by the media and by unclear messages about abuse from the greater society, parents, faculty and staff, and alumni of fraternal organizations. Many student affairs administrators reading this chapter will recall conversations with parents and alumni when the response to the dangerous use of alcohol was "thank goodness it is only booze!"

It is also clear that "entering students are not 'blank slates' on the issue of alcohol when they enroll. In fact, one-half (50%) of students are already drinking before they enroll in college" (Ishler, 2005, p. 26). Consumption of alcohol and use of other drugs has dramatically changed since parents and alumni attended college. The change in the drinking age from eighteen to twenty-one has made alcohol an illegal drug for most traditional age stu-

Developing norms and setting standards for responsible
ption of alcohol have become very difficult for student

affairs administrators as alcohol is illegal for so many students. Use of alcohol—and thus abuse—has gone underground, resulting in high consumption over short periods of time, and the institution becomes involved only when behavioral issues come to the attention of administrators.

Abuse of alcohol and other drugs can cause problems of great magnitude involving harm to both students involved in the abuse and others in the educational community. Most important, substance abuse interferes with the ability of students to meet their educational goals. Higher education in general, and student affairs in particular, has yet to develop an effective approach to the management of this issue, and student affairs continue to cope with the problems associated with illegal use and abuse of alcohol and other drugs on a regular basis.

Expectations

Since the time of the earliest colonial colleges, there has been an expectation that "something" beyond subject mastery would occur as a result of the higher education experience. Thelin (2003) indicates that colonial colleges were focused on the concept that undergraduate education should be a "civilizing experience that ensured a progression of responsible leaders for both church and state" (p. 5).

As higher education in the United States grew and diversified in many ways, including institutional purposes, curriculum, research, faculty, and facilities, changes also occurred in the expectations of students and their families for the educational experience. Whatever the change in those expectations, however, there remains a fundamental societal belief that American colleges and universities should make a positive difference in the lives of students. The National Association of Student Personnel Administrators and the American College Personnel Association in *Learning Reconsidered: A Campus-Wide Focus on the Student Experience* (2003) stated in part that "our society expects colleges and universities to graduate students who can get things done in the world and are prepared for effective and engaged citizenship" (p. 3). The process of meeting that expectation, however, provides unique challenges for students, the institution, and professional staff in student affairs.

Traditional Age Students

The expectations for the college experience of traditionally aged students have also changed over the years. Newton (2000) indicates that currently enrolled traditional age students do understand campus and community rules, for example, but they do not have a moral or personal commitment to such rules. For these students, the challenge lies in discovering ways to get around the rules. Howe and Strauss (2000) describe traditional age students as "millennials," whose expectations for college are shaped by feelings that they are special, sheltered, confident, team oriented, achieving, pressured, and conventional. These characteristics result in high expectations that the collegiate environment will be concerned with personal health and safety of students. These "millennial" students also experience high stress and a strong need to excel.

Millennial students also have a stronger connection with their parents than did previous generations, and many students rely on that connection to solve problems. Simultaneously, parents are demonstrating greater passion and a goal for perfection for the educational experience of their children at all levels (Howe and Strauss, p. 32). Cell phones and e-mail also connect students and parents much more frequently than was true of any other college generation. The result is that the relationship between parents and the institution also has evolved, with many parents becoming immediately involved in the daily problems and crisis situations involving their sons and daughters.

Expectations play a vital role in shaping the behavior of people (Bandura, 1986, Dweck and Leggett, 1988). Entering first-year students come to higher education with expectations that will shape their relationship with the collegiate environment. Kuh (1999) indicates that many of the expectations of students are not met through their first-year college experience. First-year students, for example, study, read, and write less than they expected to prior to coming to college. The expectations of entering first-year students and the values that those expectations represent also are very different from those of the faculty who teach them (Blimling and Whitt, 1999). To illustrate, three-quarters of entering first-year students value the goal of financial wealth, whereas only one-third of the faculty who teach them embrace that same goal (Sax, Astin, Amendardo, and Korn, 1996). If students are to expand their personal goals, then the expectations of faculty, staff, and the institution for their performance and success need to be stated in clear and unambiguous ways. Blimling and Whitt state that "because many more students are capable of achieving more than they imagine, it is incumbent on student affairs professionals and their faculty colleagues to nurture, cajole and challenge students to think bigger thoughts, set higher goals for their learning and personal development, and accomplish more for themselves, their families and their communities" (p. 89). The question of whether that should be the role of student affairs remains unresolved.

Non-traditional Age Students

In 2000, 40 percent of undergraduates enrolled in higher education in the United States were aged twenty-five or older (Aslanian, 2002). Almost two-thirds of adult students study on a part-time basis. The majority of adult students are women, married, and white (http://www.hispanicoutlook.com). The expectations of non-traditionally aged students for their college experience differ in many respects from those students of traditional age. Most enroll in higher education to meet a specific objective involving skill mastery, degree or certification attainment, job promotion, or meeting goals postponed because of marriage and family obligations. Aslanian indicates that although a significant number of such students will continue to seek degrees in the future, the number of adult students entering certification non-degree programs is expected to increase in the next decade. Adult students are most likely to use services such as parking, the library, computer labs, and copy machines and are less likely to use traditional student affairs programs such as health services, placement, and recreation facilities. Braxton (2003) states that "temporary enrollment intentions such as job retraining or institutional transfer are common" (p. 328) among adult students and will influence the expectations of the adult students for their collegiate experience.

The question of how student affairs will adapt programs and services for adult students remains to be answered as the age of the student population at both the graduate and undergraduate level becomes more diverse. It is also unclear whether these adaptations, if any, will help clarify the question of who holds responsibility for the lives of students.

Legal Environment

The legal environment influencing higher education and student affairs has become increasingly complex over the last three decades. Every indication is that the trend will continue into the future. Legal constraints and parameters influencing students and student affairs come from nine sources. These sources include both the federal and state constitutions, statutes at all levels, judicial decisions, the regulations and rules of government agencies, contracts, the rules of the institution, academic tradition, and foreign and international law (Barr, 2003).

Constitutional Issues

Federal constitutional protections guaranteeing freedom of religion, speech and the press, association and assembly, have been the basis for countless legal challenges to the actions taken and decisions made at public college and universities. Students at public colleges and universities also have fundamental constitutional protections against illegal searches and lack of due process in discipline matters. And they enjoy equal protection under the law. The reader is referred to Kaplin and Lee (1997), Gehring (2000), and Barr (2003) for comprehensive discussions of these constitutional issues.

Private institutions are not subject to the Federal Constitution unless the institution is engaging in state action, but "students attending such institutions do have protections" (Barr, p. 129). Some of those protections are derived from the contract of enrollment between the institution and the student. In addition, some legal protections of the individual rights of students at private institutions are protected by statutes, by the applicable state constitution, or by precedent in case law (Barr, 2003).

Liability

The legal context of responsibility for the lives of students centers more, however, on interpretation of statutes and issues of liability as reflected in court decisions. In an increasingly litigious society, it is not unusual for a student affairs administrator to be threatened with a lawsuit regarding an action taken or a decision made. The focus of many of these threatened and actual lawsuits revolves around the issue of whether the institution or the administrator has responsibility for the lives of students enrolled in the institution.

Negligence is often claimed when a student dies, is injured, is assaulted, or harms self or others. However, Gehring (2000) asserts, "To be found liable for negligence four elements must exist. First a duty must be present. Second, the duty must have been breached. Third, an injury must occur, and fourth the breach of duty must be the proximate cause of the injury" (p. 349). The question of whether a duty is owed to students is very complex, but it is central to the debate about who has responsibility for the lives of students.

Can and should the institution and thus student affairs staff act in loco parentis? Many would argue that the concept of in loco parentis is no longer viable in a society that has lowered the age of majority and has embraced rapidly changing social mores. Yet lawsuits continue to be filed claiming negligence for harm that came to a student while enrolled at a college or university. In general, the courts have recognized three general duties on the part of an institution of higher education: "to provide proper supervision, to furnish proper instruction and to maintain equipment in a reasonable state of repair" (Gehring, 2000, p. 349). For the most part, the questions of what constitutes proper instruction and keeping facilities and equipment in a state of reasonable repair may be easier to answer than the issue of what constitutes proper supervision of college students of whatever age. Is it possible to prevent a student from making either a foolish or life-threatening decision? Is it even possible for a campus to provide full security in residential units? Does the institution through employment of campus police create an atmosphere of false feelings of safety for students? The list of questions and issues could go on and on.

Determining what constitutes proper supervision of students who are of legal age has not yet been fully settled in the courts. When a student knowingly assumes the risk in an activity, it is rare that liability on the part of the institution will be found. But knowing that fact does not make student affairs administrators any more comfortable about the question of liability and responsibility for the lives of students. Although many student affairs administrators believe that "students are responsible for their own lives" (National Association of Student Personnel Administrators, 1989, p. 14), lawsuits create an atmosphere of concern. For even though it is recognized that anyone can sue anybody at any time and that the critical question is whether liability will be found, working in such a litigious environment becomes more difficult each year.

Alleged Discrimination

A second set of issues regarding responsibility for the lives of students is derived from the number of statutes and court cases in the last few decades related to the enrollment process at American colleges and universities. Title VI of the Civil Rights Act of 1964 prohibits discrimination in any program or activity receiving federal funds. Title IX of the Education Amendments of 1972 prohibits sex discrimination in those same programs, and Section 504 of the Rehabilitation Act of 1972 prohibits discrimination on the basis of handicap. These prohibitions seem to be very straightforward, but the question of what actually *is* discrimination has been litigated many times, including recent cases involving undergraduate and law school admissions criteria, financial aid awards, and intercollegiate athletics opportunities. For a full discussion of these cases, the reader is referred to the *Chronicle of Higher Education* and other periodicals for the most up-to-date information. In addition, student affairs administrators are urged to seek legal counsel, particularly when threatened by litigation. Although administrators must make decisions, legal counsel can provide an important perspective to inform such decisions.

The legal challenges to institutions of higher education are likely to continue into the future, and the outcome of those judicial decisions will inform the answer to the question of who has responsibility for the lives of students. A clear answer has not been posited by the courts regarding what duty is owed by the institution to students who abuse alcohol and other drugs, have long-term and disruptive psychological disabilities, engage in hate speech, or need expensive auxiliary aids to overcome handicapping conditions that interfere with their education. Until that occurs, student affairs administrators and others in the institution must take actions that are as fair and reasonable as possible. And they take those actions in an increasingly more restrictive financial environment.

Financial Support

"The broader fiscal context of higher education sets real constraints on what can and cannot be accomplished in any institution of higher education" (Barr, 2002, p. 7). Recent years have brought many financial challenges to the greater economy. The aftermath of terrorism attacks both in the United States and abroad combined with an interconnected world economy have created new financial challenges for the United States in all domains, including higher education. Federal and state tax revenues have been reduced while concurrently demands for services and support by the state have increased.

Public higher education institutions are facing increased competition for state funds from other areas, including but not limited to an aging infrastructure within the states, an aging population, increased demand for health care, an expanding criminal justice system, and citizen recreation. State-supported institutions are competing on a statewide level, with all of these important agenda items for support. The result has been that direct public financial support for higher education has diminished or has not kept up with inflation. Both the legislative and executive branches of state government are shifting the burden of funding from the state to the institution and its students.

Private institutions are also facing fiscal constraints. Although a relatively few private institutions cannot weather the short-term fluctuations of the economy, almost all private institutions feel the financial constraints of a changed economy. Unless the institution is well endowed, the costs of instruction are being increasingly passed on directly to students, resulting in dramatically higher costs for tuition and fees. Concurrently, legislative, parental, and student groups are expressing great concern about the rising cost of college attendance and whether access to higher education experiences has been diminished by rising costs.

Fundraising for public and private institutions also has become more challenging in recent years. During a time when both types of institutions are required to raise more money to support the enterprise, competition for philanthropic dollars has increased. Higher education is not the only game in town, and both public and private institutions are facing growing competition from museums, other levels of education, social service agencies, community action groups, the arts, and religious organizations for donations both large and small.

Also, both public and private institutions are being asked to absorb the costs of unfunded mandates from government at all levels at a time when the financial environment for higher education is becoming more restricted. Examples include the following: reporting of crime statistics, installation of sprinkler systems in residence halls, providing physical access to buildings for those with mobility issues, installing new accounting procedures, improving animal welfare in research laboratories, and so forth. The list of unfunded mandates seems to get longer each year, and it is clear that the costs to implement such mandates then must be accounted for by the institution. Governmental relief of the cost burden is not likely to happen. For a full discussion of the fiscal issues facing student affairs and higher education, see Chapter Five.

Technology has also brought increased costs during times of fiscal constraint. Students and their families have high expectations for access to technology as part of the educational environment, and technology access can be a critical factor in collegiate choice. In order to remain competitive in admissions, instruction, student life, research, and routine business transactions, institutions of higher education have invested great amounts of money in technology on many campuses. Finally, because technology is always evolving and changing, costs will continue to grow into the foreseeable future.

All of these issues are important to student affairs professionals because the increase in demand for support services, facilities, and programs in student affairs is occurring in an atmosphere of high competition and restricted resources. Something will have to give. It should be noted that although the demand for increased services for students with disabilities and those with long-term psychological concerns may be the most visible, they are only symptomatic of the problems of expanding services in order to meet real and perceived expectations of students.

The situation requires that student affairs, and the institution as a whole, discuss the core issue of whether or not, or to what extent, the institution has responsibility for the lives of students. There are, however, a number of barriers that interfere with a frank and open resolution of the issue.

Barriers

It appears that despite the old adage "you can't be all things to all people," colleges, universities, and the profession of student affairs have often attempted to do just that. Meeting all the needs and wants of students, parents, faculty, staff, and government is almost impossible in an environment of restricted or steady state resources and continued legal challenges to policies, procedures, and practices. In order to be successful in the future, a rational discussion must begin about the limitations of what an institution can and cannot do, and that discussion must include all stakeholders in the higher education enterprise, including politicians. There are, however, a number of barriers that confuse that discussion and ultimate resolution of the issue.

Attitudes of Student Affairs Professionals

Most student affairs professionals became involved in the field because of a genuine desire to help students learn, grow, and develop. That desire can at times interfere with decisions regarding realistic limitations on services. For example, if a student needs long-term therapy in order to maintain stability in the educational environment, usually staff members want to help provide that stability. Long-term therapy is labor-intensive, and resources used to help one student might be better used to assist a larger number of students in a different way. The debate regarding setting limits on the duration of therapy often focuses on the need of the individual for help rather than on a systemic solution to the funding issue and appropriate use of resources. Other solutions are possible, including mandatory student health insurance with a provision for psychological care, referral to community mental health agencies, fees for services provided to the student, or transfer of the student to another institution where help may be more readily available in the community. Often, however, such alternatives are not considered in the context of what the institution can provide. Too often, policy decisions in student affairs are primarily shaped by a strong belief that the institution *must* help *all* students *all* of the time.

Special-Interest Groups

Many colleges and universities deal with special-interest groups who strongly believe that their specific agenda should be the most important issue at the institution. Many times, special-interest groups have developed because of past discrimination or lack of access to higher education opportunity, and under those conditions such groups are highly political in nature. Each special-interest group has a strong commitment to advancing its specific agenda, and often that commitment brings challenges to the current allocation of resources, time, and energy within the institution.

Certainly, special-interest groups can be powerful, positive forces for change within the institution. Often such groups seek to make the institution and the programs and services offered therein more inclusive. The changes in the characteristics of students have caused many special-interest groups to form on college campuses. The result is continual challenges to hiring practices, admissions, curriculum, resource allocation, facilities, lack of services, and other issues. If, however, the members of the special-interest group can only see the value of their own agenda, then the question of who carries responsibility for the lives of students will become more complicated.

Denial

There are many in higher education who would deny that the issue of trying to be all things to all people is a genuine concern that must be addressed. Advocates for a particular stance will cite legal requirements, competition, and constituent interests as reasons for unbridled expansion of services despite funding concerns. But the resources of any institution can only be stretched so far, and there are real fiscal limitations regarding what most institutions can do. If Mayhew (1979) is correct when he stated that "budget is really a statement of educational purpose phrased in fiscal terms" (p. 54), then an in-depth discussion must be launched on every campus regarding the educational purposes of the institution. Further, that discussion must focus on whether meeting the needs of special-interest groups serves the educational purposes of the institution for all students.

A Sense of Entitlement

Howe and Strauss (2000) have described traditional age college students as being the most "catered to" group to ever come to American higher education. Others describe this generation of students as one with a consumer mentality. Levine and Cureton (1998) state that, in part, "students are increasingly bringing to higher education exactly the same consumer expectations they have for every other commercial enterprise with which they deal" (p. 50). From access to technology to recreation facilities to health care to instruction, students feel entitled to the best and complain when they don't receive what they perceive to be the best. Such attitudes make resolution of issues more difficult, for each student believes that his or her concern is the most important one at the institution and that the institution is obligated to respond to that concern. This sense of entitlement on the part of many students is linked to the question of who has responsibility for the lives of students. Unabated feelings of entitlement and consumerism have the potential for the institution to assume more and more responsibility for the lives of students and that could be an unintentional return to in loco parentis.

Unfunded Mandates

All too often, laws have been passed that require institutions of higher education to do something (for example, report crime statistics, increase intercollegiate athletic opportunities for women, or make programs physically accessible to all students) but provide no financial support for the mandated activity. In times of more restricted financial resources, such statutory mandates cause choices to be made, and opportunities given to some are sometimes taken away from others. To illustrate, under Title IX one criterion for compliance is proportionality of women student athletes to women student enrollment at the institution. If the athletic budget is not able to grow to cover increased participation by women, then the money must come from somewhere else—usually men's sports. So squad sizes are reduced, and over time so is scholarship money in men's sports in order to provide participation and scholarship opportunities for women. Some might say that such decisions are fine for the redress of past discrimination, but just ask the question of a student-athlete who has just had his squad size reduced or his scholarship money spread among more students if it is fair. It is critical that both the intentional and unintentional consequences of statutes passed in good faith be communicated to legislative bodies and the general public.

Suggestions for Action

The question of who is responsible for the lives of students and if there can or should be some reasonable limitations on that responsibility must be examined from at least three perspectives: philosophically, realistically, and financially. Each institution may answer the question differently because of history, tradition, or the unique mission of the institution. But it is critical that the issues be debated in the best traditions of American higher education. The following are some ideas to be considered by the profession.

1. *Student affairs should assume leadership for the needed debate.* The entire institution, including faculty, students, administrators, and the governing board needs to debate the issue of where responsibility for the lives of students is vested. Such a question cannot be answered solely by student affairs for it goes to the heart of the

educational enterprise. However, student affairs should provide the central leadership to the discussion and the resolution of the issues involved. Student affairs, historically, holds a special responsibility to examine institutional policies, procedures, practices, and priorities and determine if and how students are affected by current policies and recommended changes. Discussion of limitations on services or abandonment of traditional programs in order to serve new populations will not be a popular issue that others on the campus will embrace, but it is essential for a more rational future for higher education.

As indicated earlier, each institution may answer the question of responsibility for the lives of students very differently. Whatever the outcome, however, the debate should happen and should be intentional on the part of the institution. For if there is not an intentional debate about the question of responsibility, then the institution may fall into the trap of providing services or support because there was no clear definition of limitations or a clear philosophy dictating what can and cannot be done within that specific institutional context and mission.

2. *Clear information and facts regarding the consequences of legislation must be provided to legislators and others on a regular basis.* The debate regarding responsibility must also be taken to the halls of Congress and the state legislature. It is easy to pass bills and require action by institutions of higher education. Sometimes, however, what was passed is not what was intended or needed. For example, is it reasonable for an open access institution to have to enroll a disturbed and disturbing student for a one-credit course so that he or she can get student health insurance coverage for a long-term personal issue? Usually, such enrollments eventually contribute to rising premium costs for all students enrolled in the student health insurance program and often are accompanied by disruption of the learning environment. Is it reasonable for the institution to have to take a student to court (and engage in litigation) to stop a student from coming to class in the nude? Is it reasonable for other

students to have to have their instructional time interrupted by another who yells obscenities every three minutes and cannot stop but refuses to accept other accommodations for instruction within the campus community? These are but a few of the examples that plague student affairs administrators and institutions of higher education, and it is doubtful that legislators really envisioned any of these scenarios happening.

Student affairs professionals have an obligation to provide understandable and useful data to legislators and others in government regarding the intended and unintended consequences of statutes and regulations. Although it will take a long time, the legislative debate must happen, and institutional representatives to the legislature must be informed of the realities of unfunded statutory mandates.

3. *Regularly provide data and information on the campus*. As institutions and professional associations enter the discussion of what are the reasonable limits of responsibility for the lives of students that should be assumed by institutions, student affairs must provide data to inform the discussion. It is critical that the data given be more than anecdotal and provide real information for stakeholders to consider as the debate moves forward.

For example, the informed student affairs professional should be able to estimate the current and projected costs of dealing with students who are both disturbed and disturbing, including estimated staff hours, police response, and classroom and residence hall disruption. Further, what is the graduation rate for students who are both disturbed and disturbing? One way to confront the many dimensions of the issue is to develop an institutional impact statement of the consequences of dealing with disturbed and disturbing students. Such a statement could help those who develop statutes have a human perspective on the problem. Finally, as a profession, we should be sending one loud and consistent message to legislators about the burdens of unfunded mandates and the realities faced by students and administrators on college campus as a result of legislative actions.

4. *Encourage realism on the part of everyone.* The realism perspective must be part of the debate. What can the institution be reasonably expected to provide and at what cost? Although the doctrine of separate but equal has been struck down on racial issues, should there be a debate on whether some institutions simply have buildings that are too old to make them accessible? What educational opportunities would be lost to those with disabilities? What might be gained or lost when limited access for a few requires that funds be diverted from other pressing priorities? What other accommodations could be made for such students? These questions are representative of the harsh realities that must be faced by higher education and student affairs in the years ahead. And as uncomfortable as these discussions make student affairs professionals, they have an absolute obligation to bring this agenda forward for consideration by the educational community.

Facts must be gathered and then shared, for often decisions are made in higher education without all the facts. As the debate about the responsibility for the lives of students continues, the astute student affairs administrators will know the real costs and facts. Decisions about limitations can then be informed decisions rather than just decisions based on good wishes.

5. *Develop clear and unambiguous policies.* Finally, once the debate has been engaged and the decisions made, a clear and unambiguous stance must be adopted by the institution and by student affairs administrators. Parents and prospective students alike must clearly understand what the institution can and cannot do and why the decision was made to either limit or extend services. Such positions will not necessarily be popular, but they may be prudent and may protect the long-term responsibilities of the institution to all stakeholders of the enterprise.

6. *Seek legal advice.* As the institution and student affairs engage in these volatile and emotional debates, the legal parameters of the issues involved must be clearly understood by all parties. Seeking a legal perspective can assist the discussion and increase the

understanding of everyone involved about the risks and the benefits of any policy change.

Summary

The question about where responsibility lies for the lives of students
is central to the future of student affairs and higher education. The
discussions must occur, and there is not one easy answer for each
and every institution. So many variables are involved that campus-
based debate and discussion about what can and cannot be realistically accomplished is central to resolution of the issues involved.

Student affairs administrators must take leadership on their
campuses in confronting these complex, emotionally charged, and
difficult issues. Such discussions will not be without conflict, but
such discussions *must occur*, because the future of educational opportunities for prospective generations of students is at stake.

9

How Should Professional Associations Serve Student Affairs?

Professional associations have existed in student affairs for almost a hundred years and continue to serve important functions for institutions and individual professionals. In this chapter, the question of how these professional associations should serve student affairs in 2006 and beyond is addressed. After a brief history of the associations is presented, the profession's struggle for identity is discussed, and then various functions of student affairs professional associations are described. Current problems faced by student affairs professional associations are discussed, and a section on reframing the role of these associations is presented. The chapter concludes with some suggestions for action regarding the role of student affairs professional associations.

A Brief History

The following is a brief description of the evolution of the professional associations.

National Association of Women Deans, Administrators, and Counselors

Less than ten years after the first student affairs deans had been appointed to their positions, they realized they needed one another to advance this new field and to improve their work with students.

They were determined and compassionate educators who were often left to their own devices on their campuses to discover how best to serve the needs of students (Mathews, 1915). As new deans were appointed, they sought support and understanding from one another. This marked the beginnings of professional associations in student affairs.

Marion Talbot, the pioneering dean of women at the University of Chicago, helped establish the Association of Collegiate Alumnae and became its president in 1895–1897. This association became an organizational base for her interest in women's education and provided a model when she started organizing deans of women in 1902 (Nidiffer, 2000, p. 39). In the fall of 1903, eighteen women met in Chicago at the invitation of Talbot and her colleague, Martha Foote Crow, dean of women at Northwestern University. The meeting's official title was the "Conference of Deans of Women of the Middle West" (Potter, 1927). These meetings of women deans provided support and established standards of practice that helped to define their positions. These early deans were striving to build a profession and advance the cause of women's education. Their work eventually led to the founding of the first professional association in student affairs in 1916, the National Association of Deans of Women (Nidiffer, 2000). It evolved into the National Association of Women Deans, Administrators, and Counselors (NAWDAC) and then into the National Association for Women in Education (NAWE).

National Association of Student Personnel Administrators

In January 1919, Dean of Men Scott Goodnight of the University of Wisconsin invited deans from Minnesota, Iowa, New York, Michigan, and Illinois to meet in Madison. It was only two months after the signing of the armistice, and in Goodnight's words, "It was a time of great demoralization; it was also a very precarious time for Deans of Men, as there were so few of us" (National Association of Deans and Advisers of Men, 1938). Dean Robert Rienow of the State University of Iowa attended that first meeting of the deans of men and recalled, "We really sat around the table and bared our hearts to each other. It was in complete intimacy of confidence and each member of the conference had helpful advice from every other member. We really did get a great deal out of it. We cemented a bond of friendship there that has never been broken. We came together because correspondence was so cold, and we found common subjects, common problems. Ours was a work of service and, I think, a work of love" (National Association of Deans and Advisers of Men, 1938, p. 155). This first conference in Madison, called by Scott Goodnight, established the National Association of Deans of Men. This group eventually became the National Association of Student Personnel Administrators (NASPA).

American College Personnel Association

The founding of the National Vocational Guidance Association in 1913 led to the establishment of the National Association of Appointment Secretaries in 1924. In 1931, its name was changed to the American College Personnel Association (ACPA). ACPA later became affiliated with the American Personnel and Guidance Association (APGA), which was created in 1952 when four related associations formed a common bond to reflect their unity of purpose. ACPA's membership and orientation maintained a strong counseling base and influence; indeed, several of its presidents also served as presidents of the Division of Counseling Psychology (Division 17) of the American Psychological Association (Caple, 1985, p. 77). ACPA eventually separated from APGA and became an independent professional association in 1992.

Struggle for Identity

During the past four decades, professional associations in student affairs have multiplied, yet at the same time, they have continued to search for coherence within the higher education community.

Attempts for Unification

Not unlike adolescents seeking their identity, student affairs professional associations struggled for many years to clarify their purposes and even to define the nature of their work. Finding a common ground among many competing interests has proven quite elusive. Several attempts to forge a common purpose among student affairs groups in higher education have been made. One of the early efforts occurred in 1957, when the Inter-Association Coordinating Council was formed (Bloland, 1972). When the Council of Student Personnel Associations (COSPA) was formed in 1963, it was labeled the most promising development in the past thirty years (Cowley, 1964). In 1970, ACPA, NASPA, and NAWDAC met to consider the possibility of a single professional association for student affairs. As late as 2003, another effort was made to consolidate ACPA and NASPA (Coomes, Wilson, and Gerda, 2003). However, all of these efforts to form one "umbrella" professional association have failed. The very different histories of these professional associations, the specialized priorities of their members, and their unique purposes have proven to be formidable obstacles to consolidation.

Proliferation of Specialized Associations

At the same time that the major professional associations were struggling, without success, to unify the student affairs field, there was a rapid proliferation of new professional groups within student affairs, as the field continued to grow and expand. Now, with over thirty-five national professional associations within student affairs, this development could be viewed as a sign of strength, with new specialties formed to meet the changing needs of students and institutions. But it could also be viewed as a serious threat to the field, resulting in fragmentation. The traditional commitment of the field to the whole student seemed to be contradicted by this specialization in student affairs. This rapid expansion of these many groups raised questions about how professional associations should serve institutions and students (Sandeen, 1998).

Collaborations

The American College Personnel Association and the National Association of Student Personnel Administrators have emerged as the two *generalist* professional groups for the student affairs profession. Their memberships include hundreds of institutions and thousands of individual professionals. With national offices staffed with association executives and with educational programs, services, conferences, seminars, institutes, commissions, state and regional organizations, publications, Web sites, research projects, foundations, and international activities, ACPA and NASPA have developed far beyond what Marion Talbot and Scott Goodnight could have ever imagined a hundred years ago! Although both associations strive to be inclusive in their membership and purposes, large numbers of student affairs professionals identify primarily with associations that represent their special interests, such as financial aid, career development, judicial affairs, recreational sports, orientation, and college unions. With some thirty-five national professional associations representing the special interests of various groups, the student affairs field has been harshly criticized for its lack of coherence and its inability to agree on its major purposes (for example, Bloland, 1972; Fenske, 1989; Brubacher and Rudy, 1976). This has raised additional questions about what these organizations are actually designed to do.

Functions of Student Affairs Professional Associations

Policy, Professional Development, Research

Student affairs professional associations are highly dependent upon volunteers, who not only make association policy but also plan and conduct most of the programs, seminars, and conferences sponsored by the associations. Research projects are often undertaken, and the results are disseminated to the members; public policy statements may be made on important higher education issues; standards for good practice in the profession may be promulgated; career improvement programs may be offered; standards for professional preparation may be issued; professional development institutes may be conducted; professional journals, books, and monographs may be published; extensive information about the field may be provided via Web sites; and international activities may be organized (Nuss, 2000). One of the most important functions that professional associations continue to provide, of course, is the opportunity for members to interact and to share their common concerns.

Collaboration

Although efforts to merge the major student affairs associations have not been successful, effective collaboration among associations has resulted in some very important advances in the field. The Joint Statement on Rights and Freedoms of Students (American Association of University Professors and others, 1967); the Council for the Advancement of Standards in Higher Education (2003); the Standards of Good Practice in Student Affairs (Blimling and Whitt, 1999); and *Learning Reconsidered: A Campus-Wide Focus on the Student Experience* (National Association of Student Personnel Administrators, American College Personnel Association, 2004) are illustrations of how cooperation among associations can contribute to improvements in higher education.

Accreditation

Accreditation of graduate preparation programs in student affairs has also been an issue debated within professional associations for many years. The Council for the Accreditation of Counseling and Related Educational Programs (CACREP) established accreditation standards for student affairs graduate preparation programs in 1981 ("About CACREP," 2003). Perhaps because of CACREP's close affiliation with the American Counseling Association, these standards have not met with as much acceptance as have those issued by the Council for the Advancement of Standards in Higher Education (*Standards and Guidelines for Masters-Level Preparation of Student Affairs Professionals* [2003]). But the professional associations themselves have stopped short of acting as official accreditation bodies for student affairs graduate preparation programs. A recent draft proposal to the NASPA Board of Directors on the development of a *national registry* for student affairs professionals (Janosik, 2002) attracted some attention, but the lack of enthusiasm for the proposal was most likely an indication that the student affairs field is still too diverse and too fragmented to accept any model it may find constricting to its highly varied purposes.

Serving Institutions

Do student affairs professional associations make any difference? Does anyone outside student affairs really care or pay attention to what these associations do? Based upon the enthusiasm of the members, these associations seem to be quite valuable to them. This may be a sufficient reason for their existence, but most of them recognize that they have other important roles—improving their own institutions and the overall quality of higher education. Student affairs professional associations have served their own members quite well but have not done as well in serving their institutions. They have also fallen short in making substantive contributions to the improvement of higher education. There are several issues the student affairs professional associations need to address.

Current Problems with Student Affairs Professional Associations

Current Strengths

Most student affairs professional associations are now more active than ever in providing services and support to their members. Moreover, their membership is strong and their financial health is good, especially those that have institutional dues as the basis of their operations. Several associations have established private foundations to augment the programs and services they provide, many are actively engaged in securing grants from external sources, and others collaborate with related professional associations in higher education, especially those located in Washington, D.C. The Internet has opened up new opportunities for professional associations to provide programs and services to their members, especially ones involving professional development. As the student affairs field continues to expand, and even more specialized professional associations are established (for example, the Association for Multicultural Counseling and Development and the Association for Gay, Lesbian, and Bisexual Issues in Counseling), it is obvious that practicing professionals need to talk with one another. What then is the problem?

Lack of Focus on the Whole Student

The most serious problem resulting from the astonishing proliferation of specialty professional associations in student affairs is that it has made a mockery of the most important historical idea of the profession: a commitment to the whole student. The resulting fragmentation now occurring within the field is reminiscent of what happened to the undergraduate curriculum decades ago, when rapid expansion of academic disciplines obliterated any intellectual coherence in what students were taught. It may be ironic that student affairs emerged in the 1890s partially as a reaction to faculty specialization, and now, only about a century later, student affairs has become a victim of its own specialization. By doing so, it is dangerously abandoning the very idea that is the reason for its existence—the education of the whole student. The motives of the various specialty student affairs associations are laudatory—to serve their members' needs effectively; they are not the problem. The problem is that this focus on more and more narrow aspects of the student via professional associations has encouraged staff members on campus to concentrate their efforts on single-issue concerns or characteristics of students. Treating students as whole persons has always been the strength of student affairs; moving away from this important principle can fragment the profession and seriously restrict the impact of student affairs on the campus. The growing number of specialty student affairs associations may be innocent participants in this process, but in their zeal to form new groups that will give more visibility to their own needs and agendas, they may be contributing to a diminishing of the field.

Narrow Focus on Parochial, Guild-Based Goals

Student affairs professional associations have focused most of their efforts on meeting the needs of their members, and they have done this very well. They are among the most successful professional associations in securing volunteer leadership for the various programs and services they conduct. Moreover, they often have served their members so well that lasting personal and professional friendships have resulted from their activities. Some student affairs professionals may become so involved in their professional association that they gain more satisfaction and appreciation from their professional association than they do from their work on their own campus! However, student affairs professional associations have focused their efforts far too often on parochial, guild-related concerns. Their emphasis has been directed inwardly instead of outwardly to the larger higher education community. It may be important to professionals in student affairs associations to argue about membership services, the structure of the central office, or the proper definition of multiculturalism, but in focusing primarily on such matters, the associations often forgo their chance to make useful contributions to the improvement of higher education. This inward focus of student affairs professional associations has at times seemed like an intentional escape from the rough and tumble world of higher education—in a relaxed, isolated, and secure atmosphere, professionals can speak their own special language with others who not only understand but will actually listen! This is not unique to student affairs associations, of course, and it most likely has considerable therapeutic value for the participants. But this inward focus has too often deprived student affairs professional associations from being listened to very seriously by the rest of the higher education community.

Lack of an Effective, Coordinated Voice in Higher Education

Because of the proliferation of student affairs associations, each claiming to represent a special constituency or agenda within the field, it has been very difficult for student affairs to speak with an effective voice in higher education. Even though the two generalist associations, ACPA and NASPA, have collaborated on some issues in recent years (for example, National Association of Student Personnel Administrators, American College Personnel Association, 2004; Schroeder and Associates, 1996), there is no consensus about what the student affairs profession advocates on the most important issues being debated in higher education. As a result, the views and insights of student affairs leaders are not heard, or in other cases, only the views of the specialty associations are heard. Along with academic affairs, development, and financial affairs, student affairs now represents one of the major administrative components of most colleges and universities; however, the views of the profession are seldom represented in any state or national higher education debates. The reason for this is that the various student affairs associations cannot form any kind of meaningful consensus on the most important issues. As a result, their voice is either not heard, or the message is questioned because its source credibility is in doubt. Student affairs is no longer merely a support service on most campuses, content to operate on the periphery of the academic enterprise; it is now a vital part of the learning process at many colleges and universities. But the profession's message will become confusing and ambiguous if it is perceived by the higher education community as little more than a maze of competing, self-serving, and uncoordinated associations.

Need to Address Concerns of Campus Presidents

Successful senior student affairs officers understand that the support of their presidents is the most important single factor in the success of their campus programs and services (Sandeen, 2001b).

College and university presidents are charged by their boards to improve their institutions, and of course, hire senior student affairs officers who can assist them in achieving their various goals. Most presidents understand and are supportive of the role of professional associations for their faculty and staff but are also quite skeptical about the ever-increasing number of them, which can contribute to more specialization on the campus. They are also increasingly concerned with the costs of professional associations for their institutions and are skeptical of what the benefits for the institution might be. Most of all, they are often irritated by the poorly concealed attempts by some specialized professional associations to influence the policies or priorities of their institutions (Dickeson, 1999; Cowley, 1980). For example, if a professional association suggests to an institution that the ratio of professional staff to students in a particular area is in "violation" of its standard, presidents and provosts may tire quickly of this overused tactic to influence the allocation of resources. In some cases, such naive suggestions by specialized professional associations can actually do more harm than good. Because there are so many student affairs professional associations, presidents may not pay much attention to the scattered views being expressed by them; this can be embarrassing and awkward for senior student affairs officers when the president asks, "Who is speaking for whom?" Presidents are likely to be supportive of professional associations that help them achieve their institutional goals. Student affairs associations have focused too exclusively on the individual needs of their members and not enough on the needs of the institutions they serve.

NASPA and ACPA Challenges

The many specialized student affairs professional associations have formed primarily because the two generalist associations in the field, ACPA and NASPA, have not been able to respond effectively to the needs of these professional staff. Although ACPA and NASPA purport to serve all professionals in student affairs, those who work in financial aid, counseling, academic advising, admissions,

housing, career services, health services, recreational sports, orientation, judicial affairs, student activities, and several other areas do not
agree and have opted to form their own groups to meet their needs.
The huge expansion of student affairs is certainly responsible for
much of this fragmentation, but it is mainly a failure of the two
umbrella groups to achieve what they have been advocating for many
years—an integrated, inclusive student affairs program. Both ACPA
and NASPA have made efforts to reach out to professionals in the
various specialties, but for the most part, this has not been successful.
In particular, ACPA and NASPA have fallen short in meeting the
needs of student affairs professionals in the fifteen hundred community colleges. Senior student affairs officers have been traditionally
more likely to identify professionally with NASPA, although many
of them are also affiliated with ACPA. Senior student affairs officers
understand that their own campus student affairs programs must be
inclusive and integrated—the various departments and offices they
have created are not independent entities. Yet in their own professional associations, they have been unable to achieve this same inclusiveness and integration. Changing demographics, new technology,
and new types of institutions present ACPA and NASPA with additional challenges, making their efforts to represent all student affairs
professionals even more difficult. Until ACPA and NASPA can truly
represent the needs of all professionals, the student affairs field will
be viewed by the rest of the higher education community as disunited
and fragmented. Now is an appropriate time to reconsider how professional associations serve the profession and higher education.

Reframing the Role of Professional Associations in Student Affairs

Student Affairs Is Now a Mature Field

The student affairs field may not have achieved the formal desig-
nation of a profession in 2006, but it has expanded greatly in the
past forty years and now is a recognized and essential part of

the administrative and service structure of colleges and universities. Its leaders are vital contributors to the education of students and active participants in policymaking in academic, research, development, and financial affairs at their institutions. Student affairs professionals no longer need to view themselves only as support personnel, acting outside the mainstream activity of the campus. By their professional preparation, their experience, and their knowledge of student involvement and development, they are making substantive contributions to student learning. They have earned their place in the campus community, and in 2006, opportunities have never been better for them to have a positive impact on the quality of student life and learning. This new self-confidence within student affairs is reflected in the activities of the best practitioners on the campuses, and now, the major student affairs professional associations should seize this opportunity and act upon it! The publication of *The Student Learning Imperative* (Schroeder and Associates, 1996) is an example of the kind of positive activity that has already demonstrated what student affairs professional associations can contribute to the larger higher education community.

A Need to Be Heard on Broader Issues

Student affairs associations have been heard on important issues such as student rights, campus crime, student records, and substance abuse; such activity should continue. But they also should be heard on issues such as the core curriculum, student-faculty relations, student learning communities, and the improvement of teaching. Student affairs has matured significantly in the past four decades, and the expanded roles its leaders have achieved on the campuses should now be reflected in the activities and priorities of student affairs professional associations.

Working with Mainstream Higher Education Associations

Collaboration between academic affairs and student affairs has become almost commonplace on the campuses in recent years and represents a very positive development. Student affairs professional associations and academic affairs associations, such as the Association for the Study of Higher Education (ASHE), the National Association of State Universities and Land-Grant Colleges (NASULGC), the National Association of Independent Colleges and Universities (NAICU), and the American Council on Education (ACE), are already cooperating in some joint projects, and this activity is very encouraging. Efforts to work more closely with the American Association of Community Colleges (AACC) may result in increased participation by student affairs professionals from these two-year institutions in ACPA and NASPA. Because student affairs leaders work so closely with their financial and development colleagues on the campuses, establishing cooperative programs with the National Association of College and University Business Officers (NACUBO) and the Council for the Advancement and Support of Education (CASE) could yield positive results for student affairs. The major associations in student affairs (ACPA and NASPA) should take the lead in expanding such collaborative relationships.

The Continuing Debate About Merging ACPA and NASPA

A good deal of time and energy has been expended during the past three decades debating the feasibility of a merger of ACPA and NASPA. There may be some benefit to continue this debate within the field, but it should be understood that such a merger itself is not the important issue. The critical issue is how persuasive student affairs leaders can be on their own campuses in contributing to the improvement of student life and learning. The major professional associations, whether merged or not, must have this as their primary goal. While still serving the individual needs of their members, their primary goal should be to assist institutions in improving their educational and service programs. There is nothing harmful about merging major associations—but those involved in such efforts should not fool themselves into thinking that such a merger will automatically produce any new or encouraging results for the field.

What is needed—merger or not—is for student affairs professional associations to develop programs and take actions that will enable their individual members and institutions to improve the quality of learning on the campuses.

Need for a Coherent Student Affairs Voice in Higher Education

Some thirty years ago, the Council of Student Affairs Professional Associations (COSPA) failed to achieve its goals of bringing some coherence and unity to the student affairs field. When it disappeared after its short existence, not many people seemed to care. Since that time, the lack of coherence and the disunity have increased, as many additional specialty student affairs associations have been established. This expansion and specialization has robbed student affairs of an effective and coherent voice within the higher education community. There is still significant disagreement on what the priorities of the field should be, what the best professional preparation should be, and what the fundamental purposes of the field should be. Until such time as ACPA and NASPA can forge a sufficient consensus about these important issues, the effective voice of student affairs in higher education will be seriously limited. The student affairs field does not need an orthodoxy or set of fixed ideas—it has demonstrated that it can embrace many differences—but it cannot expect to have an important role in the larger higher education community unless its major professional associations can speak in a consistent and coherent manner on behalf of the field. Reviving and retrying the COSPA model may be worthy of consideration as a way to pursue this important goal.

A Recommitment to the Whole Student

The Student Personnel Point of View (American Council on Education, 1937) served as the foundation document for the student affairs field for many years. Its revision after World War II (American Council on Education, 1949) provided additional guidance for student affairs professionals, as did a fiftieth anniversary edition published in 1987 (National Association of Student Personnel Administrators, 1987). Since that time, a number of new statements have been published through the auspices of the professional associations in student affairs (for example, Schroeder and Associates, 1996; National Association of Student Personnel Administrators and others, 1998; National Association of Student Personnel Administrators, 2001). These efforts represent some of the most thoughtful and valuable accomplishments by leaders in student affairs, working through their professional associations. However, even these fine efforts have not been able to stop the splintering of the field into even more specialized associations, along with the interests, priorities, and agendas they represent. The education of the whole student remains the fundamental idea of student affairs, and this idea forms the basis for all of the major documents published over the years by ACPA and NASPA. If it is lost, or if it is allowed to be dismantled by a host of more specialized agendas, then the voice of student affairs in the higher education community will be greatly diminished. It is the responsibility of the leaders of ACPA and NASPA to see that this fundamental idea of the education of the whole student remains the primary thrust of the field.

A Daunting Challenge

Given the American penchant to form organizations, it is highly unlikely that the growth of specialty professional associations in student affairs will ever stop. This same proliferation of specialized associations has occurred in almost every academic discipline in American higher education over the years, and there are no signs that it is diminishing. It certainly has made it more difficult to build and sustain general education programs for undergraduates, especially at large universities. As faculty interests become more and more specialized and as faculty identify professionally with associations that represent and celebrate their specialties, the task of finding any common ground in what undergraduates should learn becomes more daunting. It has taken the student affairs field a longer time to duplicate this same process within its own field, but with over thirty-five professional associations (not including dozens of regional and state groups) in 2006, it is now experiencing the same fragmentation and loss of coherence that has occurred in most academic disciplines. The consequences for the student affairs field and, more important, for the education of students can be very serious. Who will take the responsibility to educate the whole student? Are the student affairs field and its major professional associations willing to stand idle and witness the disintegration of its basic commitments? Will the major student affairs professional associations be content to have the student dissected by gender, race, ethnicity, age, physical ability, career interests, place of residence, financial background, religion, sexual orientation, or psychological type in a manner whereby no one is treating students as a whole? The best student affairs practitioners now recognize that the several labels given to students over the years (and the many associations formed to confirm them) can become obstacles to good education and personal development on the campus. It is time for the major professional associations to affirm what practitioners have learned on the campus and to readdress the education of the whole student.

Professional associations in student affairs are of course a reflection of their members and their needs for continuing learning, information sharing, new ideas, and even friendship. They should represent the aspirations and ideals of their members, pushing them to grow and to achieve higher levels of competence in their work.

Suggestions for Action

Student affairs professional associations should accept their responsibility to reach out to the larger world of higher education, knowing that they are representing ideas that are unique and critical to good student learning. The most important responsibility of student affairs professional associations is to communicate a coherent and persuasive message to the higher education community.

Student affairs professional associations have an important role to play in helping individuals grow and learn, but their primary role should be to help colleges and universities improve learning conditions for students. The needs of institutions should be the primary focus of their activities and programs. And senior student affairs officers, as representatives of their institutions to professional associations, should ensure that this occurs.

As the student affairs field has matured in the past three decades, a large number of specialized professional associations have formed. Student affairs leaders should strive to prevent the fragmentation of the profession that this proliferation of specialized associations may come to represent. The most powerful and important concept in the field remains the education of the whole student, and if the message of student affairs to the larger higher education community is diluted, its impact will be greatly diminished.

Merging ACPA and NASPA into one association may be a concept worthy of continuing discussion, but the focus should be upon leadership within the profession, representation of institutions, and especially upon how student affairs can best present its message to the larger higher education community. Senior student affairs officers should take the lead in this discussion, assuring their campus presidents and senior academic affairs officers that whatever changes take place will benefit their institutions and student learning.

The world of higher education is changing rapidly, and the focus on student learning, made all the more exciting with the incredible advances in technology, is resulting in more collaboration. This also means that many of the former boundaries in higher education are becoming irrelevant. For many years, professional associations have staked out their own areas of concern, evidenced by the specialized interests they have represented on their own campuses. But these old divisions in higher education are becoming more blurred each year, and this change certainly will soon be reflected in higher education professional associations.

Student affairs leaders in NASPA and ACPA should collaborate with other higher education professional associations to find new ways to improve student learning. Perhaps the most important topic concerning mergers of professional associations ought to be an exploration of a newly created association, bringing together professionals in student affairs, academic affairs, and assessment. Student affairs leaders should take the initiative in such discussions.

Professional associations in student affairs continue to play a vital role in the development of the field. They have greatly expanded over the past decades and reflect the current emphasis on specialization and member services. Student affairs professional associations face a number of challenges and are now in an excellent position to be effective participants in higher education's efforts to improve the education of students.

References

Adan, A., and Felner, R. D. "Ecological Congruence and Adaptation of Minority Youth During Their Transition to College." *Journal of Community Psychology*, 1995, *23*, 256–269.

Adelman, C. "Diversity: Walk the Walk, and Drop the Talk." *Change*, 1997, *29* (4), 35–45.

Allen, J., and Bresciani, M. J. "Public Institutions, Public Challenges." *Change*, 2003, *35*, (1), 20–23.

Ambler, D. A. "Designing and Managing Programs: The Administrator Role." In U. Delworth and G. R. Hanson (eds.), *Student Services: A Handbook for the Profession*. (2nd ed.) San Francisco: Jossey-Bass, 1989.

Ambler, D. A. "Developing Internal Management Structures." In M. J. Barr and Associates (eds.), *The Handbook of Student Affairs Administration*. San Francisco: Jossey-Bass, 1993.

Ambler, D. "Organization and Administrative Models." In M. J. Barr, M. K. Desler, and Associates. (eds.)., *The Handbook of Student Affairs Administration*. (2nd. ed.) San Francisco: Jossey-Bass, 2000.

American Association for Higher Education. "Nine Principles of Good Practice for Assessing Student Learning." *Assessment Forum*. 2004.

American Association of University Professors, U.S. National Student Association, American Council on Education. *The Student Personnel Point of View*. Washington, D.C.: ACE, 1937.

American Association of University Professors, U.S. National Student Association, Association of American Colleges, National Association of Student Personnel Administrators, National Association of Women Deans and Counselors. *Joint Statement on Rights and Freedoms of Students*. Washington, D.C.: AAUP, 1967.

American College Personnel Association. *The Student Learning Imperative*. Washington, D.C.: ACPA, 1994.

American College Testing Program. "Collegiate Assessment of Academic Proficiency (Calif.)." Iowa City, Iowa: American College Testing Program, 2000.

American Council on Education. *The Student Personnel Point of View*. American Council on Education Studies. Series 1, Vol. 1, No. 3. Washington, D.C.: American Council on Education, 1937.

American Council on Education, Committee on Student Personnel Work. *The Student Personnel Point of View*. (revised ed.) American Council on Education Studies. Series 6, No. 13. Washington, D.C.: American Council on Education, 1949.

Appleton, J. "The Context." In P. Moore (ed.), *Managing the Political Dimensions of Student Affairs*. New Directions for Student Services, no. 55. San Francisco: Jossey-Bass, 1991.

Aronowitz, S. *The Knowledge Factory: Dismantling the Corporate University and Creating the Higher Learning*. Boston: Beacon Press, 2000.

Aslanian, C. C. *Adult Students Today*. New York: College Board, 2002.

Association of American Colleges. *Integrity in the College Curriculum: A Report to the Academic Community*. Washington, D.C.: AAC, 1985.

Astin, A. W. *Four Critical Years: Effects of College on Beliefs, Attitudes and Knowledge*. San Francisco: Jossey-Bass, 1977.

Astin, A. W. *Achieving Educational Excellence*. San Francisco: Jossey-Bass, 1985.

Astin, A. W. *Assessment for Excellence*. New York: American Council on Education, Macmillan, 1991.

Astin, A. W. *What Matters in College: Four Critical Years Revisited*. San Francisco: Jossey-Bass, 1997.

Astin, A. W. "Diversity and Multiculturalism on the Campus: How Are Students Affected?" *Change*, 1993, 25 (2), 44–49.

Astin, A. W., Dey, E. L., and Korn, W. W. *The American Freshman: Twenty-five Year Trends, 1966–1990*. Los Angeles: Higher Education Research Institute, 1991.

Baldridge, J. *Power and Conflict in the University: Research in the Sociology of Campus Organizations*. New York: Wiley, 1971.

Bandura, A. *Social Foundations of Thought and Action: A Social Cognitive Theory*. Upper Saddle River, N.J.: Prentice Hall, 1986.

Banning, J. H. (ed.). *Campus Ecology: A Perspective for Student Affairs*. Cincinnati, Ohio: National Association of Student Personnel Administrators. 1978.

Banning, J. H., and Strange, C. C. *Educating by Design: Creating Campus Learning Environments That Work*. San Francisco: Jossey-Bass, 2001.

Banta, T. W. *Making a Difference: Outcomes of a Decade of Assessment in Higher Education*. San Francisco: Jossey-Bass, 1993.

Banta, T. W. *Building a Scholarship of Assessment*. San Francisco: Jossey-Bass, 2002.

Banta, T. W., and Kuh, G. D. "A Missing Link in Assessment: Collaboration Between Academic and Student Affairs Professionals." *Change*, 1998, *30* (2) 40–46.

Barker, R. *Ecological Psychology: Concepts for Studying Human Behavior*. San Francisco: Jossey-Bass, 1968.

Barr, M. J. "Growing Staff Diversity and Changing Career Paths." In M. J. Barr, M. L. Upcraft, and Associates (eds.), *New Futures for Student Affairs*. San Francisco: Jossey-Bass, 1990.

Barr, M. J. "Organizational and Administrative Models." In M. J. Barr, M. K. Desler, and Associates (ed.), *The Handbook of Student Affairs Administration*. San Francisco: Jossey-Bass, 1993.

Barr, M. J. *Academic Administrator's Guide to Budgets and Financial Management*. San Francisco: Jossey-Bass, 2002.

Barr, M. J. "Legal Foundations of Student Affairs Practice. In S. R. Komives, D. B. Woodard Jr., and Associates (eds.), *Student Services: A Handbook for the Profession*. (4th ed.) San Francisco: Jossey-Bass, 2003.

Barr, M. J., Upcraft, M. L., and Associates. (eds.). *New Futures for Student Affairs: Building a Vision for Professional Leadership and Practice*. San Francisco: Jossey-Bass, 1990.

Bartem, R., and Manning, S. "Outsourcing in Higher Education." *Change*, 2001, *33* (1), 42–47.

Bartlett, T. "What's Wrong With Harvard?" *Chronicle of Higher Education*, May 7, 2004, pp. A14–A16.

Baxter-Magolda, M. B. *Knowing and Reasoning in College: Gender Related Patterns in Students' Intellectual Development*. San Francisco: Jossey-Bass, 1992.

Belch, H. A. (ed.). *Serving Students with Disabilities*. New Directions for Student Services, no. 91. San Francisco: Jossey-Bass, 2000.

Bender, B. "Job Satisfaction in Student Affairs." *NASPA Journal*, 1980, *18*, 2–9.

Benton, S. A., and others. "Changes in Counseling Center Client Problems Across 13 Years." *Professional Psychology Research and Practice*, *34* (1), 66–72, 2003.

Blackhurst, A. "Career Satisfaction and Perceptions of Sex Discrimination Among Women Student Affairs Professionals. *NASPA Journal*, 2000, *37*, 399–413.

Blackhurst, A. E., Brandt, J. B., and Kalinowski, J. G. "Effects of Career Development on the Organizational Commitment and Life Satisfaction of Women Student Affairs Administrators." *NASPA Journal*, 1998 *36* (1), 19–34.

Blimling, G. S., Whitt, E. J., and Associates (eds.). *Good Practice in Student Affairs: Principles to Foster Student Learning.* San Francisco: Jossey-Bass, 1999.

Bloland, P. A. "Ecumenicalism in College Student Personnel." *Journal of College Student Personnel,* 1972, *13,* 102–111.

Blumenstyk, G., and Farrell, E. F. "In For-Profit Higher Education, Buying Binge Heats Up." *Chronicle of Higher Education,* July 11, 2003.

Bok, D. "Reclaiming the Public Trust." *Change,* 1992, 24, 4, 13–19.

Bok, D. *Universities in the Marketplace: The Commercialization of Higher Education.* Princeton, N.J.: Princeton University Press, 2003.

Bok, D., and Bowen, W. G. *The Shape of the River: Long-Term Consequences of Considering Race in College Admissions.* Princeton, N.J.: Princeton University Press, 2002.

Bonham, G. "A Moral Imperative." *Change,* 1983, *15* (1), 14–15.

Borrego, A. M. "A Wave of Consolidation Hits For-Profit Higher Education." *Chronicle of Higher Education,* August 10, 2001.

Bowen, H. *Investment in Learning: The Individual and Social Value of American Higher Education.* San Francisco: Jossey-Bass, 1979.

Boyer, E. L. *Campus Life: In Search of Community.* San Francisco: The Carnegie Foundation for the Advancement of Teaching, 1990.

Bradfield, C. D., and Myers, R. A. "Enriching the Student Learning Experience through Community Service Training." *About Campus,* 1996, *1* (1), 28–29.

Braxton, J. M. "Student Success." In S. R. Komives, D. B. Woodard Jr., and Associates (eds.), *Student Services: A Handbook for the Profession.* (4th ed.) San Francisco: Jossey-Bass, 2003.

Breneman, D. W., and Taylor, A. L. *Strategies for Promoting Excellence in a Time of Scarce Resources.* San Francisco: Jossey-Bass, 1996.

Bresciani, M. J., and others. "In Search of Meaningful and Manageable Assessment: Academic Program Review at North Carolina State University." In T. W. Banta. *Assessment Update.* Number 6. San Francisco: Jossey-Bass, 2002.

Brogue, E. G. "An Agenda of Common Caring: The Call for Community in Higher Education." In W. M. McDonald and Associates (eds.), *Creating Campus Community: In Search of Ernest Boyer's Legacy.* San Francisco: Jossey-Bass, 2002.

Brown, R. D. *Student Development in Tomorrow's Higher Education: A Return to the Academy.* Washington, D.C.: American Personnel and Guidance Association, 1972.

Brown, R. D. "Creating an Ethical Community." In H. Canon and R. D. Brown (eds.), *Applied Ethics in Student Services.* New Directions for Student Services, no. 30. San Francisco: Jossey-Bass, 1985.

Brown, R. D. "Professional Pathways and Professional Education." In L. V. Moore and R. D. Young (eds.), *Expanding Opportunities for Professional Education*. New Directions for Student Services, no. 37. San Francisco: Jossey-Bass, 1987.

Brown, R. D. *Performance Appraisal as a Tool for Staff Development*. New Directions for Student Services, no. 43. San Francisco: Jossey-Bass, 1988.

Brubacher, J. S., and Rudy, W. *Higher Education in Transition: A History of American Colleges and Universities*. New Brunswick, N.J.: Transaction, 1976.

Burd, S. "For-Profit Colleges Want a Little Respect." *Chronicle of Higher Education*, September 5, 2003.

Burke, J. C., and Serban, A. M. *Performance Funding for Public Higher Education: Fad or Trend?* New Directions for Institutional Research, no. 97. San Francisco: Jossey-Bass, 1998.

Canon, H. "Maintaining High Ethical Standards." In M. J. Barr and Associates (ed.), *The Handbook of Student Affairs Administration*. San Francisco: Jossey-Bass, 1993.

Canon, H., and Brown R. (eds.). *Applied Ethics in Student Services*. New Directions in [for] Student Services, no. 30. San Francisco: Jossey-Bass, 1985.

Caple, R. B. "Diversity." *Journal of College Student Development*. 1990, *31* (4), 291–292.

Caple, R. B. *To Mark the Beginning: A Social History of Student Affairs*. Lanham, Md.: University Press of America and American College Personnel Association, 1998.

Carnegie Council on Policy Studies in Higher Education. *Three Thousand Futures: The Next Twenty Years for Higher Education. Final Report of the Carnegie Council on Policy Studies in Higher Education*. San Francisco: Jossey-Bass, 1980.

Carnevale, D. "Should Distance Students Pay for Campus Based Services?" *Chronicle of Higher Education*, September 14, 2001.

Carney, C. C. *Native American Higher Education in the United States*. New Brunswick, N.J.: Transaction, 1999.

Chaffee, E. E. *Rational Decision Making in Higher Education*. Boulder, Colo.: National Center for Higher Education Management Systems, 1983.

Chang, M. J. "Is It More Than About Getting Along? The Broader Educational Relevance of Reducing Students' Racial Biases." *Journal of College Student Development*, 2001, *42* (2), 93–105.

Chickering, A. W. *Education and Identity*. San Francisco: Jossey-Bass, 1969.

Chickering, A. W., and Associates. *The Modern American College: Responding to the Realities of Diverse Students and a Changing Society*. San Francisco: Jossey-Bass, 1981.

Chickering, A. W., and Gamson, Z. F. *Applying the Seven Principles for Good Practice in Undergraduate Education*. San Francisco: Jossey-Bass, 1991.

Chickering, A. W., and Reisser, L. *Education and Identity*. (2nd ed.) San Francisco: Jossey Bass, 1993.

Christie, R., and Ragans, S. (1999) "Beyond Borders: A Model for Student and Staff Development." In J. Dalton (ed.), *Beyond Borders: How International Developments Are Changing Student Affairs Practice*. New Directions for Student Services, no. 86, San Francisco: Jossey-Bass, 1999.

Chronicle of Higher Education. *Chronicle of Higher Education Almanac*, 2003, *50* (1).

Clark, B. *Creating Entrepreneurial Universities: Organizational Pathways of Transformation*. New York: Pergamon Press, 1998.

Cohen, M., and Marsh, J. "A Garbage Can Model of Organizational Choice." *Administrative Science Quarterly, 17* (1) 1–25, 1972.

Coles, R. "Hispanic Dreams/American Dreams." *Change*, 1988, *20* (3), 12–13.

Coomes, M. D., Wilson, M. E., and Gerda, J. J. *Of Visions, Values, and Voices: Consolidating ACPA and NASPA*. Paper distributed for public discussion, Bowling Green State University, Bowling Green, Ohio, 2003.

Cortes, C. E. "The Diversity Within: Intermarriage, Identity, and Campus Community." *About Campus*, 2000, *2* (5), 5–10.

Council for the Accreditation of Counseling and Related Education Programs. "About CACREP." [www.counseling.org/cacrep/default.htm]. 2003.

Council for the Advancement of Standards in Higher Education. *Standards and Guidelines for Masters-Level Preparation of Student Affairs Professionals*. Washington, D.C.: American College Student Personnel Association, 2003.

Council for the Advancement of Standards in Higher Education. *Standards and Guidelines*. Washington, D.C.: Council for the Advancement of Standards in Higher Education, 2003.

Council for the Advancement of Standards in Higher Education. *Standards and Guidelines for Student Services Development Programs*. Washington, D.C.: American College Personnel Association, 2003.

Courts, P. L., and McInerney, K. H. *Assessment in Higher Education: Politics, Pedagogy, and Portfolios*. Westport, Conn.: Praeger, 1993.

Cowley, W. H. "Reflections of a Troublesome but Hopeful Rip Van Winkle." *Journal of College Student Personnel*. 1964, 6 (2), 66-73.

Cowley, W. H. *Presidents, Professors, and Trustees*. Washington, D.C.: Jossey-Bass, 1980.

Cross, W. "Black Identity: Rediscovering the Distinction Between Personal Identity and Reference Group Orientation." In M. Spencer, G. Brookins, and W. Allen (eds.), *Beginnings: The Social and Affective Development of Black Children*. Hillsdale, N.J.: Erlbaum, 1985.

Cuyjet, M. J. (ed.). *Helping African-American Men Succeed in College*. New Directions for Student Services, no. 80. San Francisco: Jossey-Bass, 1997.

Dalton, J. C. "Managing Human Resources." In D. B. Woodard, S. R. Komives, and Associates (eds.), *Student Services: A Handbook for the Profession*. (4th ed.) San Francisco: Jossey-Bass, 2003.

Davis, T. M. (ed.). *Open Doors 1996/97: Report on International Educational Exchange*. New York: Institute on International Education, 1997.

DeAlva, J. "Remaking the Academy." *Educause*, March/April, 2000, pp. 32–40.

Delco, W. "Testing From a Legislative Perspective." In R. T. Alpert, W. P. Garth, and R. G. Allan (eds.), *Assessing Basic Academic Skills in Higher Education: The Texas Approach*. Hillsdale, N.J.: Erlbaum, 1989.

Delworth, U. *Dealing With the Behavioral and Psychological Problems of Students*. New Directions for Student Services, no. 45. San Francisco: Jossey-Bass, 1989.

Dickeson, R. C. *Prioritizing Academic Programs and Services: Reallocating Resources to Achieve Strategic Balance*. San Francisco: Jossey-Bass, 1999.

Drucker, P. *Managing in the Next Society*. New York: Truman Talley Books, 2002.

Dweck, C. A., and Leggett, E. L. "A Social Cognitive Approach to Maturation and Personality." *Psychological Review*, 95 (2), 256–273, 1988.

Eddy, E. D. *The College Influence on Student Character*. Washington, D.C.: American Council on Education, 1959.

Edgerton, R. "An Assessment of Assessment." In Educational Testing Service. *Assessing the Outcomes of Higher Education*. Princeton, N.J.: Educational Testing Service, 1987.

Edgerton, R. *Education White Paper*. [www.pewtrusts.com.] 1999.

Education Commission of the States. *Quality Assurance in Undergraduate Education: What the Public Expects*. Denver, Colo.: ECS, 1994.

El-Khawas, E. "The Many Dimensions of Diversity." In D. B. Woodard Jr., S. R. Komives, and Associates (eds.). *Student Services: A Handbook for the Profession*. (4th ed.) San Francisco: Jossey-Bass, 2003.

Erikson, E. "Identity and the Life Cycle." *Psychological Issues Monograph*. 1 (1), 1–171. Madison, Conn.: International Universities Press, 1959.

Ern, E. H. "Managing Resources Strategically." In M. J. Barr and Associates (eds.), *The Handbook of Student Affairs Administration*. San Francisco: Jossey-Bass, 1993, p. 453.

Erwin, T. D. *The NPEC Sourcebook on Assessment: Definitions and Assessment Methods for Critical Thinking, Problem Solving, and Writing.* Washington, D.C.: U.S. Department of Education, Office of Educational Research and Improvement, 2000.

Evans, N. J. "Attrition of Student Affairs Professionals: A Review of the Literature." *Journal of College Student Development,* 1988, *29,* 25–29.

Evans, N., and Phelps Tobin, C. (eds.). *State of the Art of Preparation and Practice in Student Affairs: Another Look.* New York: Rowen and Littlefield, 1998.

Ewell, P. T. *Student Tracking: New Techniques, New Demands.* San Francisco: Jossey-Bass, 1995.

Ewell, P. T. "Assessment of Higher Education Quality: Priorities and Politics." In S. J. Messick (ed.), *Assessment in Higher Education: Issues of Access, Quality and Student Development.* Rahway, N.J.: Erlbaum, 1999.

Ewell, P. T. "Assessment Again." *Change,* 2003, *35* (1), 4.

Eyermann, I., and Sanlo, R. "Documenting Their Existence: Lesbian, Gay, Bisexual and Transgender Students on Campus." In R. Sanlo, S. Rankin, and R. Schoenberg (eds.), *Our Place on Campus: Lesbian, Gay, Bisexual and Transgender Services and Programs in Higher Education.* Westport, Conn.: Greenwood Press, 2002.

Feagin, J. R. *The Agony of Education: Black Students at White Colleges and Universities.* New York: Routledge, 1996.

Feldman, K., and Newcomb, T. *The Impact of College on Students.* San Francisco: Jossey-Bass, 1969.

Fenske, R. H. "Evolution of the Student Services Profession." In U. Delworth and G. R. Hanson (eds.), Student Services: A Handbook for the Profession. San Francisco: Jossey-Bass, 1989, pp. 25–56.

Flowers, L. A., and Howard-Hamilton, M. F. "A Qualitative Study of Graduate Students' Perceptions of Diversity Issues in Student Affairs Preparation Programs." *Journal of College Student Development,* 2002, *43* (1), 199–123.

Ford, D. *Resources: Personal Counseling.* [www.wcet.info/projects/]. 2000.

Forrest, L. "Guiding, Supporting, and Advising Students: The Counselor Role." In U. Delworth and G. R. Hanson (eds.), *Student Services: A Handbook for the Profession.* (2nd ed.) San Francisco: Jossey-Bass, 1989.

Fox, M., Lowe, S., and McClellan, G. *Serving Native-American Students.* New Directions for Student Services, no. 109. San Francisco: Jossey-Bass, 2005.

Freedman, J. O. "Ghosts of the Past: Anti-Semitism at Elite Colleges." *Chronicle of Higher Education,* December 1, 2000, pp. B7–10.

Freeman, M. A., Nuss, E. M., and Barr, M. J. "Meeting the Need for Staff Diversity." In M. J. Barr and Associates (eds.). *The Handbook of Student Affairs Administration*. San Francisco: Jossey-Bass, 1993.

Fried, J. "Maintaining High Ethical Standards." In M. J. Barr, M. K. Desler, and Associates (eds.). *The Handbook of Student Affairs Administration*. (2nd ed.) San Francisco: Jossey-Bass, 2000.

Fried, J., and Associates. *Shifting Paradigms in Student Affairs*. Lanham, Md.: University Press of America/American College Personnel Association, 1995.

Friedman, T. L. *The World Is Flat: A Brief History of the 20th Century*. New York: Farrar, Straus & Giroux, 2005.

Gaff, J. G., and Ratcliff, J. L. (eds.). *Handbook of the Undergraduate Curriculum: A Comprehensive Guide to Purposes, Structures, Practices, and Change*. San Francisco: Jossey-Bass, 1996.

Gaither, G., Nedwek, B. P., and Neal, J. E. *Measuring Up: The Promise and Pitfalls of Performance Indicators in Higher Education*. ASHE-ERIC Higher Education Report: Number 5. Washington, D.C.: George Washington University Graduate School of Education and Human Development, 1994.

Gallagher, R. P., and Zhang, B. *National Survey of Counseling Center Directors 2002*. Pittsburgh, Pa.: International Association of Counseling Center Directors, 2003.

Gardner, J. N., and Upcraft, M. L. *The Freshman Year Experience: Helping Students Survive and Succeed in College*. San Francisco: Jossey-Bass, 1989.

Gardner, J. N., and Van der Veer, G. *The Senior Year Experience: Facilitating Integration, Reflection, Closure, and Transition*. San Francisco: Jossey-Bass, 1998.

Gates, S. M., and others. *Ensuring Quality and Productivity in Higher Education: An Analysis of Assessment Practices*. ASHE-ERIC Higher Education Report: Volume 29, Number 1, San Francisco: Jossey-Bass, 2002.

Gehring, D. D. "Understanding the Legal Implications of Student Affairs Practice." In M. J. Barr, M. K. Desler, and Associates (eds.), *The Handbook of Student Affairs Administration*. San Francisco: Jossey-Bass, 2000.

Gilligan, C. "In a Different Voice: Women's Perceptions of Self and Morality." *Harvard Educational Review, 47*, 418–437, 1977.

Gothin, V. "From Diagnosis to Treatment: Addressing Legal Issues Related to Mental Illness on Your Campus." Paper presented at the Stetson University Law Conference, Tampa, Fla., 2003.

Gould, E. *The University in a Corporate Culture*. New Haven, Conn.: Yale University Press, 2003.

Gratz v. Bollinger. (2003), 539 U.S.

Grutter v. Bollinger. (2003), 539 U.S.

Hardee, M. D. "Personnel Services for Improving the Campus Climate of Learning." *Journal of the National Association of Women Deans and Counselors.* April, 1961, *24,* 122-127.

Heath, D. "A Model of Becoming a Liberally Educated and Mature Student." In C. Parker (ed.), *Encouraging Development in College Students.* Minneapolis: University of Minnesota Press, 1978.

Heath, D. *Growing Up in College.* San Francisco: Jossey-Bass, 1968.

Hebel, S. "Appeals Court Backs Fee System." *Chronicle of Higher Education,* October 11, 2002.

Hebel, S. "SUNY's Board Approves Plan for System-wide Tests of Undergraduates." *Chronicle of Higher Education,* June 23, 2004, p. 21.

Helms, J. (ed.). *Black and White Racial Identity: Theory, Research and Practice.* Westport, Conn.: Greenwood Press, 1990.

Holland, J. *The Psychology of Vocational Choice: A Theory of Personality Types and Model Environments.* Waltham, Mass.: Blaisdell, 1966.

Holland, J. *Making Vocational Choices: A Theory of Vocational Personalities and Work Environments.* Upper Saddle River, N.J.: Prentice Hall, 1985.

Hollingsworth, K., and Dunkle, J., "Dealing with Disturbed and Disturbing Students: Best Practices and Their Implications." Paper presented at the National Association of Student Personnel Administrators Annual Conference, Tampa, Fla.: 2005.

Holmes, D. R., Verrier, D., and Chisholm, P. "Persistence in Student Affairs Work: Attitudes and Job Shifts Among Master's Program Graduates." *Journal of College Student Personnel,* 1983, *24,* 438–443.

Hopkins, E. H. "The Essentials of a Student Personnel Program." (Originally published, 1948). In G. L. Saddelmire and A. L. Rentz (eds.), (1986). *Student Affairs: A Profession's Heritage.* Alexandria, Va.: American College Personnel Association,

Hopkins, R. *Educating Black Males: Critical Lessons in Schooling, Community, and Power.* Albany, N.Y.: State University of New York Press, 1977.

Hossler, D. "The Problem with College Rankings." *About Campus,* 2000, *5* (1), 20–24.

Hossler, D., and Bean, J. B. *The Strategic Management of College Enrollments.* San Francisco: Jossey-Bass, 1990.

Howard-Hamilton, M. "Theory to Practice: Applying Developmental Theories Relevant to African-American Men." In M. Cuyjet (ed.), *Helping African-American Men Succeed in College.* New Directions for Student Services, no. 80. San Francisco: Jossey-Bass. 1997.

Howe, N., and Strauss, W. *Millennials Rising: The Next Generation*. New York: Vintage Books, 2000.

Hoy, W., and Miskel, C. *Educational Administration: Theory, Research and Practice*. New York: Random House, 1978.

Hsia, J., and Hirono-Nakanishi, M. "The Demographics of Diversity: The Asian and Pacific American Experience." *Change*, 1989, *21* (5), 20–27

Hughes, R. "The Fraying of America." *Time*, February 3, 1992, pp. 44–49.

Hune, S. "Demographics and Diversity of Asian-American College Students." In M. McEwen, C. M., and others. *Working with Asian American College Students*. New Directions for Student Services, no. 97. San Francisco: Jossey-Bass, 2002.

Hurst, J. C. "The Matthew Shepard Tragedy: Management of a Crisis." *About Campus*, 1999, *5* (3), 5–11.

Hurst, J. C., Morrill, W. H., and Oetting, E. R. (eds.). *Dimensions of Intervention for Student Development*. New York: Wiley, 1980.

Hurtado, S. *Enacting Diverse Learning Environments: Improving the Climate for Racial/Ethnic Diversity in Higher Education*. Washington, D.C.: George Washington University, 1999.

Hutchings, P., and Marchese, T. "Watching Assessment: Questions, Stories, Prospects." *Change*, 1990, *22* (5), 12–38.

Hyman, R. "Creating Campus Partnerships for Student Success." *College and University*, 1995, *71* (2) 2–8.

Ishler, J. L. "Today's First Year Students." In M. L. Upcraft, J. N. Gardner, B. O. Barefoot, and Associates (eds.), *Challenging and Supporting the First-Year Student*. San Francisco: Jossey-Bass, 2005.

Jackson, M. L. "Fund Raising and Development." In M. J. Barr and M. K. Desler (eds.), *The Handbook of Student Affairs Administration*. (2nd ed.) San Francisco: Jossey-Bass, 2000. pp. 597–611.

Jacob, P. E. *Changing Values in College*. New York: Harper, 1957.

Janosik, S. M. "The Development and Implementation of a National Registry for Student Affairs Administrators." Draft Proposal presented to the NASPA Board of Directors, January 19, 2002.

Johnstone, S., Ewell, P., and Paulson, K. *Student Learning as Academic Currency*. American Council on Education, Center for Policy Analysis: [www.acenet.edu/bookstore/pdf/distributed-learning/distributed-learning-04.pdf]. 2002.

Kantor, R. M., and Stein, B. A. *Life in Organizations*. New York: Basic Books, 1979.

Kaplin, W. A., and Lee, B. A. *A Legal Guide for Student Affairs Professionals*. San Francisco: Jossey-Bass, 1997.

Katz, J., and Associates. *No Time for Youth: Growth and Constraint in College Students*. San Francisco: Jossey-Bass, 1969

Kellogg, K. *Collaboration: Student Affairs and Academic Affairs Working Together to Promote Student Learning*. ERIC-Higher Education Digest Series. Washington, D.C.: George Washington University, 1999.

Kellom, G. *Developing Effective Student Services Programs for College Men*. New Directions for Student Services, no. 107. San Francisco: Jossey-Bass, 2004.

Kerr, T. *Academic Advising*. [www.wcet.info/projects/laap/resources/ac_ad.asp]. 2002.

Kilgore, D., and Rice, P. J. (eds.). *Meeting the Special Needs of Adult Students*. New Directions for Student Services, no. 102. San Francisco: Jossey-Bass, 2003.

Kinley, E. "Implementing Distance Education, the Impact of Institutional Characteristics: A View from the Department Chair's Chair." Unpublished doctoral dissertation. University of Nebraska-Lincoln, 2001.

Kirp, D. L. "Higher Education, Inc.: Avoiding the Perils of Outsourcing." *Chronicle of Higher Education*, March 15, 2002.

Kitchener, K. S. "Ethical Principles and Ethical Decisions in Student Affairs." In H. Canon and R. Brown (eds.), *Applied Ethics in Student Services*. New Directions for Student Services, no. 30. San Francisco: Jossey-Bass, 1985.

Kitchener, K. S., and King, P. "The Reflective Judgment Model: Concepts of Justification and Their Relationship to Age and Education." *Journal of Applied Developmental Psychology*, 1981 *2*, 89–116, 1981.

Kohlberg, L. "Stage and Sequence: The Cognitive-Development Approach to Socialization." In D. Goslin (ed.), *Handbook of Socialization Theory*. Skokie, Ill.: Rand McNally, 1969.

Komives, S. R. "The Changing Nature of Work in Higher Education." In C. S. Johnson and H. E. Cheatham (eds.), *Higher Education Trends for the Next Century: A Research Agenda for Student Success*. Washington, D.C.: American College Personnel Association, 1999.

Komives, S. R., and Woodard, D. B., and Associates. *Student Services: A Handbook for the Profession*. (4th ed.) San Francisco: Jossey-Bass, 2003.

Kotter, M. C. "Restructuring Student Services: A Philosophical Framework." In D. B. Woodard Jr. (ed.), *Budgeting as a Tool for Policy in Student Affairs*. San Francisco: Jossey-Bass, 1995, pp. 5–13.

Kramer, M., and Weiner, S. S. *Dialogues for Diversity: Community and Ethnicity on Campus*. Phoenix, Ariz.: Oryx Press, 1994.

Kruger, K. "On-line Student Services: Where Is Your Campus?" *Leadership Exchange*. Washington, D.C.: National Association of Student Personnel Administrators, fall 2003, pp. 23–24.

Kuh, G. D. "Organizational Concepts and Influences." In U. Delworth, G. Hanson, and Associates (eds.), *Student Services: A Handbook for the Profession.* (2nd ed.) San Francisco: Jossey-Bass, 1989.

Kuh, G. D. "Guiding Principles for Creating Seamless Learning Environments for Undergraduates." *Journal of College Student Development*, 1996, *2*, 135–148.

Kuh, G. D. "Working Together to Enhance Student Learning Inside and Outside the Classroom: New Looks or Same Old Story?" In *Assessing Impact: Evidence and Action—Presentations from the 1997 ASHE Conference on Assessment and Quality.* Washington, D.C.: American Association for Higher Education, 1997.

Kuh, G. D. "Setting the Bar Higher to Promote Student Learning." In G. S. Blimling, E. J. Whitt, and Associates (eds.), *Good Practice in Student Affairs: Principles to Foster Student Learning.* San Francisco: Jossey-Bass, 1999.

Kuh, G. D. "Assessing What Really Matters to Student Learning." *Change*, 2001, *33* (3), 10–19.

Kuh, G. D. "Organizational Theory." In S. R. Komives, D. B. Woodard Jr., and Associates (eds.), *Student Services: A Handbook for the Profession.* (4th ed.) San Francisco: Jossey-Bass. 2003.

Kuh, G. D. "What We're Learning About Student Engagement from NSSE" *Change*, 2003, *35* (2), 24–33.

Kuh, G. D., Kinzie, J., Schuh, J. H., Whitt, E. J., and Associates. *Student Success in College: Creating Conditions that Matter.* San Francisco: Jossey-Bass, 2005.

Kuh, G. D., Lyons, J., Miller, T., and Trow, J. *Reasonable Expectations: Renewing the Educational Contract Between Institutions and Students.* Washington, D.C.: National Association of Student Personnel Administrators, 1995.

Kuh, G. D., Schuh, J. H., and Whitt, E. J. *Involving Colleges: Successful Approaches to Fostering Student Learning and Development Outside the Classroom.* San Francisco: Jossey Bass, 1991.

Lark, J. S. "Lesbian, Gay, and Bisexual Concerns in Student Affairs: Themes and Transitions in the Development of the Professional Literature." *NASPA Journal*, 1998, *25* (2), 157–168.

Latham, S., and Dalton, J.C. *International Skills and Experiences for a Global Future.* In J. C. Dalton (ed.), *Beyond Borders: How International Developments are Changing Student Affairs Practices.* New Directions for Student Services, no. 86., 1999.

Lemann, N. *The Big Test: The Secret History of the American Meritocracy.* New York: Farrar, Straus & Giroux, 1999.

Leonard, E. A. *Origins of Personnel Services in American Higher Education.* Minneapolis: University of Minnesota Press, 1956.

Levine, A., and Cureton, J. *When Hope and Fear Collide: A Portrait of Today's College Students.* San Francisco: Jossey-Bass, 1998.

Levine, D. O. *The American College and the Culture of Aspiration, 1915–1940.* Ithaca, N.Y.: Cornell University Press, 1986.

Light, R. J. "Listening to Students." *About Campus,* 2000, 7 (3), 17–22.

Lloyd-Jones, E. *Student Personnel Work at Northwestern University.* New York: Harper, 1929.

Lloyd-Jones, E., and Smith M. R. *Student Personnel Work as Deeper Teaching.* New York: Harper and Brass, 1954.

Loevinger, J. *Ego Development: Conceptions and Theories.* San Francisco: Jossey-Bass, 1976.

Lorden, L. P. "Attrition in the Student Affairs Profession." *NASPA Journal,* 1998, 35 (3), 207–216.

Love, P. G., and Estanek, S. M. *Rethinking Student Affairs Practice.* San Francisco: Jossey Bass, 2004.

Lubinescu, E. S., Ratcliff, J. L., and Gaffney, M. A. "Two Continuums Collide: Accreditation and Assessment." In J. L. Ratcliff, E. S. Lubinescu, and M. A. Gaffney (eds.), *How Accreditation Influences Assessment.* New Directions for Higher Education, no. 133. San Francisco: Jossey-Bass, 2001.

Magolda, M. B., and Porterfield, W. D. *Assessing Intellectual Development: The Link Between Theory and Practice: A Comprehensive Assessment Program.* Washington, D.C.: American College Personnel Association. 1993.

Malaney, G. D. "The Structure and Function of Student Affairs Research Offices." In G. D. Malaney (ed.), *Student Affairs Research, Evaluation, and Assessment: Structure and Practice in a Time of Change.* New Directions for Student Services, no. 85. San Francisco: Jossey-Bass, 1999.

Marcia, J. "Development and Validation of Ego-Identity Status." *Journal of Personality,* 1966, 3, 551–558.

Massy, W. F. "Auditing Higher Education to Improve Quality." *Chronicle of Higher Education Review,* June 20, 2003, p. B-16.

Mathews, L. K. *The Dean of Women.* Cambridge: Riverside Press, 1915.

Mayhew, L. B. *Surviving the Eighties: Strategies and Procedures for Solving Fiscal and Enrollment Problems.* San Francisco: Jossey-Bass, 1979.

McClellan, G. S., Fox, M. T., and Lowe, S. C. "Where We Have Been: A History of Native-American Higher Education." In M. T. Fox, S. C. Low, and G. S. McClellan (eds.), *Serving Native-American Students.* New Directions for Student Services, no. 109. San Francisco: Jossey-Bass. 2004.

McClellan, S. A. "Development of the Multicultural Assessment of Campus
     Programming Questionnaire." *Measurement and Evaluation in Counseling
     and Development,* 1996, *29* (2), 86–99.

McCune, P. "What Do Disabilities Have to do with Diversity?" *About Campus,*
     2001, 6 (2), 5–12.

McEwen, M. K. *Working with Asian American College Students.* San Francisco:
     Jossey-Bass, 2002.

McEwen, M. K., and others. *Working with Asian-American College Students.* New
     Directions for Student Services, no. 97. San Francisco: Jossey-Bass, 2003.

Meara, N., Schmidt, L., and Day, J. "Principles and Virtues: A Foundation for
     Ethical Decisions, Policies and Character." *Counseling Psychologists.* 1996,
     24 (1) 1–72.

Mentkowski, M., and Associates. *Learning That Lasts: Integrating Learning Devel-
     opment and Performance in College and Beyond.* San Francisco: Jossey-Bass,
     2000.

Menlove, R. Hansford, D., and Lignugaris-Kraft, B. *Creating a Community of Dis-
     tance Learners: Putting Technology to Work.* Conference paper presented at
     Capitalizing Leadership in Rural Special Education. (ERIC Document
     Reproduction Service, NO ED439890), 2000.

Messick, S. J. (ed.). *Assessment in Higher Education: Issues of Access, Quality,
     Student Development, and Public Policy.* Mahwah, N.J.: Erlbaum, 1999.

Miller, T., Bender, B., Schuh, J., and Associates. *Promoting Reasonable Expectations:
     Aligning Student and Institutional Expectations of the College Experience.* San
     Francisco: Jossey-Bass, 2005.

Mills, D. B., and Barr, M. J. "Private Versus Public Institutions: How Do Finan-
     cial Issues Compare?" In J. H. Schuh (ed.), *Financial Management for Stu-
     dent Affairs Administrators.* Alexandria, Va.: American College Personnel
     Association, 1990.

Moore, P. "The Political Dimensions of Decision Making." In M. J. Barr,
     M. K. Desler, and Associates (eds.), *The Handbook of Student Affairs
     Administration.* (2nd ed.) San Francisco: Jossey-Bass, 2000.

Moos, R. H. *Evaluating Educational Environments: Procedures, Measures, Findings
     and Policy Implications.* San Francisco: Jossey-Bass, 1979.

Morison, S. E. *Three Centuries of Harvard, 1636–1936.* Cambridge: Harvard
     University Press, 1936.

Mueller, K. H. *Student Personnel Work in Higher Education.* Boston: Houghton
     Mifflin, 1961.

Myers, I. *Introduction to Type.* Palo Alto, Calif.: Consulting Psychologists Press,
     1980.

National Association of Deans and Advisers of Men. *Proceedings of the Twentieth Annual Conference*. Madison, Wis.: NADAM, 1938, p. 155.

National Association of Student Personnel Administrators. *A Perspective on Student Affairs: A Statement Issued on the 50th Anniversary of the Student Personnel Point of View*. Washington, D.C.: NASPA, 1987.

National Association of Student Personnel Administrators. "A Perspective on Student Affairs." In *Points of View*, Washington, D.C.: NASPA, 1989.

National Association of Student Personnel Administrators. *Reasonable Expectations: Renewing the Educational Compact Between Institutions and Students*. Washington, D.C.: NASPA, 2001.

National Association of Student Personnel Administrators. *Leadership for Diversity Institute: Creating A Campus to Which People Want to Belong*. E-Learning Conference, February 2004.

National Association of Student Personnel Administrators, American Association for Higher Education, and American College Personnel Association. *Powerful Partnerships: Shared Responsibilities for Student Learning*. Washington, D.C.: ACPA, 1998.

National Association of Student Personnel Administrators, American College Personnel Association. "Learning Reconsidered: A Campus-Wide Focus on the Student Experience." Unpublished paper. Washington D.C.: National Association of Student Personnel Administrators, 2003.

National Association of Student Personnel Administrators, American College Personnel Association. *Learning Reconsidered: A Campus-Wide Focus on the Student Experience*. Washington, D.C.: NASPA, ACPA, 2004.

National Center for Postsecondary Improvement. "A Report to Stakeholders on the Condition and Effectiveness of Postsecondary Education. Part One: The Recent College Graduate." *Change*, 2001a, *33* (3), 28–42.

National Center for Postsecondary Improvement. "A Report to Stakeholders on the Condition and Effectiveness of Postsecondary Education. Part Two: The Public." *Change*, 2001b, *33* (5), 23–38.

National Center for Postsecondary Improvement. "A Report to Stakeholders on the Condition and Effectiveness of Postsecondary Education. Part Three: Employers." *Change*, 2002, *34* (1), 23–38.

National Educational Goals Panel. *The National Education Goals Report*. Washington, D.C.: National Education Goals Panel, 1991.

National Governors Association. *Time for Results: The Governors' Report on Education*. Washington, D.C.: The National Governors' Association, 1986.

National Institute on Education. Study Group on the Conditions of Excellence in American Higher Education. *Involvement in Learning: Realizing the Potential of American Higher Education*. Washington, D.C.: U.S. Government Printing Office, 1984.

Newcomb, T. M. *College Peer Groups*. Chicago: Aldine de Gruyter, 1966.

Newton, F. B. "The New Student." *About Campus*, Washington, D.C.: American College Personnel Association, 2000.

Nidiffer, J. *Pioneering Deans of Women: More Than Wise and Pious Matrons*. New York: Teachers College Press, 2000.

Nuss, E. M. "The Role of Professional Associations." In M. J. Barr and M. K. Desler (eds.), *The Handbook of Student Affairs Administration*. (2nd ed.) San Francisco: Jossey-Bass, 2000, pp. 492–507.

Nuss, E. M. "The Development of Student Affairs." In S. R. Komives, D. B. Woodard Jr., and Associates (eds.), *Student Services: A Handbook for the Profession*. (4th ed.) San Francisco: Jossey-Bass, 2003.

Ortiz, A. M. (ed.). *Addressing the Unique Needs of Latino American Students*. New Directions for Student Services, no. 105. San Francisco: Jossey-Bass, 2004.

Ortiz, A. M. "Promoting the Success of Latino Students: A Call for Action." In A. M. Ortiz (ed.), *Addressing the Unique Needs of Latino Students*. New Directions for Student Services, no. 105. San Francisco: Jossey-Bass, 2004.

Pace, C. *Measuring Outcomes of College: Fifty Years of Findings and Recommendations for the Future*. San Francisco: Jossey-Bass, 1979.

Pace, C., and Stern, G. An Approach to Measuring the Psychological Characteristics of College Environments. Journal of Educational Psychology, 1958, 49, 269–277, 1958.

Palomba, C. A., and Banta, T. W. *Assessment Essentials: Planning, Implementing, and Improving Assessment in Higher Education*. San Francisco: Jossey-Bass, 1999.

Palomba, C. A., and Banta, T. W. (eds.). *Assessing Student Competence in Accredited Disciplines: Pioneering Approaches to Assessment in Higher Education*. Sterling, Va.: Stylus Publishing, 2001.

Parker, C. (ed.). *Encouraging Development in College Students*. Minneapolis: University of Minnesota Press, 1978.

Pascarella, E. T. (ed.). *Studying Student Attrition*. San Francisco: Jossey-Bass, 1982.

Pascarella, E. T., Edison, M., Nora, A., Hagedorn, L., and Terenzini, P. "Influence on Students' Openness to Diversity and Challenge in the First Year of College." *Journal of Higher Education*, 1996, 67, 174–195.

Pascarella, E. T., and Terenzini, P. T. *How College Affects Students*. San Francisco: Jossey-Bass, 1991.

Pascarella, E. T., and Terenzini, P. T. *How College Affects Students. Volume Two: A Third Decade of Research*. San Francisco: Jossey-Bass, 2005.

Patankar, M. "A Rule-Based Expert System Approach to Academic Advising." *Innovations in Education and Training International*, 1998, 35 (1) 49–58.

Pembroke, W. J. "Fiscal Constraints on Program Development." In M. J. Barr, L. A. Keating, and Associates (eds.), *Developing Effective Student Services Programs*. San Francisco: Jossey-Bass, 1985, p. 101.

Penietz, B. "Community College Students Perceptions of Student Services When Enrolled In Telecourses." *Dissertation Abstracts International*. (UMI no. 735008), 1997.

Penney, S. W., and Rose, B. B. *Dollars for Dreams: Student Affairs Staff as Fund Raisers*. Washington, D.C.: National Association of Student Personnel Administrators, 2001.

Penny, J. F. "Student Personnel Work: A Profession Stillborn." *The Personnel and Guidance Journal*. June, 1969, 47, 10, 958-962.

Perry, W. "Cognitive and Ethical Growth." In A. Chickering and Associates (eds.), *The Modern American College: Responding to the New Realities of Diverse Students and a Changing Society*. San Francisco: Jossey-Bass, 1981.

Perry, W. *Forms of Intellectual and Ethical Development in the College Years: A Scheme*. Austin, Tex.: Holt, Rinehart and Winston, 1970.

Pickering, J. W., and Hanson, G. R. (eds.). *Collaboration Between Student Affairs and Institutional Researchers to Improve Institutional Effectiveness*. New Directions for Institutional Research, no. 108. San Francisco: Jossey-Bass, 2000.

Polite, V. C., and Davis, J. E. (eds.). *African-American Males in School and Society*. New York: Teachers College Press, 1999.

Pope, R., Reynolds, A., and Mueller, J. *Multicultural Competence in Student Affairs*. San Francisco: Jossey-Bass, 2004.

Potter, M. R. "Report of Committee on History of the National Association of Deans of Women." *National Association of Deans of Women Yearbook*. 1927.

Pruitt-Logan, A. S., and Isaac, P. D. (eds.). *Student Services for the Changing Graduate Population*. New Directions for Student Services, no. 72. San Francisco: Jossey-Bass, 1995.

Ragle, J., and Justice, S. "The Disturbing Student and the Judicial Process." In U. Delworth (ed.), *Dealing with the Behavioral and Psychological Problems of Students*. New Directions for Student Services, no. 45. San Francisco: Jossey-Bass, 1989.

Ratcliff, J. L. *Putting Students at the Center of Statewide Assessment Plans*. University Park, Pa.: National Center on Postsecondary Teaching, Learning, and

Assessment. Washington, D.C.: U.S. Department of Education. Office of Educational Research and Improvement, 1995.

Rayman, J. *The Changing Role of Career Services*. New Directions for Student Services, no. 62. San Francisco: Jossey-Bass, 1993.

Regents of the *University of California v. Bakke*, (1978) 438 U.S. 265.

Rhatigan, J. J. "The History and Philosophy of Student Affairs." In M. J. Barr, M. K. Desler, and Associates (eds.), *The Handbook of Student Affairs Administration*. (2nd ed.) San Francisco: Jossey-Bass, 2000.

Rhoades, G. "Rising, Stratified Administrative Costs: Student Services' Place." In D. B. Woodard Jr. (ed.), *Budgeting as a Tool for Policy in Student Affairs*. San Francisco: Jossey-Bass, 1995, pp. 25–37.

Richmond, J., and Sherman, K. "Student-Development Preparation and Placement: A Longitudinal Study of Graduate Students' and New Professionals' Experiences." *Journal of College Student Development*, 1991 32, 8–16.

Rosenblum, K., and Travis, T. C. (eds.). *The Meaning of Difference: American Constructions of Race, Sex and Gender, Social Class, and Sexual Orientation: A Text/Reader*. Boston: McGraw-Hill, 2000.

Rudolph, F. *The American College and University: A History*. New York: A. Knopf, 1962.

Rudolph, F. *The American College and University: A History*. New York: Vintage Books, 1965.

Sagaria, M. D., and Johnsrud, L. K. "Mobility Within the Student Affairs Profession." *Journal of College Student Development*, 1988 29, 30–40.

Sandeen, A. "A Chief Student Affairs Officers Perspective on the AISP Model." In U. Delworth (ed.), *Dealing with the Behavioral and Psychological Problems of Students*. New Directions for Student Services, no. 45. San Francisco: Jossey-Bass, 1989.

Sandeen, A. *The Chief Student Affairs Officer: Leader, Manager, Mediator, Educator*. San Francisco: Jossey Bass, 1991.

Sandeen, A. "Creeping Specialization in Student Affairs." *About Campus*, 1998, 3 (2), 2–3.

Sandeen, A. *Making a Difference: Profiles of Successful Student Affairs Leaders*. Washington, D.C.: NASPA, 2001a.

Sandeen, A. "Organizing Student Affairs Divisions." In R. B. Winston, Jr., D. G. Creamer, and T. K. Miller (eds.), *The Professional Student Affairs Administrator: Educator, Leader, and Manager*. New York: Brunner/Mazel, 2001b.

Sanford, N. *The American College: A Psychological and Social Interpretation of Higher Learning*. New York: Wiley, 1962.

Sanford, N. *Where Colleges Fail: A Study of the Student as a Person*. New York: Wiley, 1967.

Sanlo, R. L. *Unheard Voices: The Effects of Silence on Lesbian and Gay Educators*. Westport, Conn.: Greenwood Press, 1999.

Sanlo, R. L., Rankin, S., and Schoenberg, R. (eds.). *Our Place on Campus: Lesbian, Gay, Bisexual, Transgender Services and Programs in Higher Education*. Westport, Conn.: Greenwood Press, 2002.

Sax, L. J., Astin, A. W., Amendardo, M., and Korn, W. D. *The American College Teacher: National Norms for the 1995–96 HERI Faculty Survey*. Los Angeles: University of California Research Institute. 1996.

Schein, E. *Organizational Culture and Leadership*. (2nd ed.) San Francisco: Jossey-Bass, 1992.

Schilling, K. L., and Schilling, K. M. "Looking Back, Moving Ahead: Assessment in the Senior Year." In J. Gardner, G. Van der Veer, and Associates (eds.), *The Senior Year Experience: Facilitating Integration, Reflection, Closures, and Transition*. San Francisco: Jossey-Bass, 1998.

Schmidt, P. "Academe's Hispanic Future." *The Chronicle of Higher Education*, November 28, 2003, pp. A8–A12.

Schroeder, C. S., and Associates. *The Student Learning Imperative: Implications for Student Affairs*. Washington, D.C.: American College Personnel Association, 1996.

Schroeder, C. S., and Hurst, J. C. "Designing Learning Environments That Integrate Curricular and Co-curricular Experiences." *Journal of College Student Development*, 1996, *37* (2), 174–181.

Schuh, J. H. "Fiscal Pressures on Higher Education and Student Affairs." In M. J. Barr (ed.), *The Handbook of Student Affairs Administration*. San Francisco: Jossey-Bass, 1993, pp. 49.

Schuh, J. H., and Bender, B. E. (eds.). *Using Benchmarking to Inform Practice in Higher Education*. San Francisco: Jossey-Bass, 2002.

Schuh, J. H., and Rickard, S. T. "Planning and Budgeting." In U. Delworth and G. H. Hansson (eds.), *Student Services: A Handbook for the Profession*. (2nd ed.) San Francisco: Jossey-Bass, 1989, pp. 461.

Schuh, J. H., and Whitt, E. J. *Creating Successful Partnerships Between Academic and Student Affairs*. New Directions for Student Services Sourcebook, no. 87. San Francisco: Jossey-Bass, 1999.

Secretarial Notes. *Sixth Annual Conference of Deans and Advisers of Men*. University of Michigan, NADAM, 1924, p. 9.

Sedlacek, W. E. *Beyond the Big Test: Non-Cognitive Assessment in Higher Education*. San Francisco: Jossey-Bass, 2004.

Shapiro, D., and Shulman, C. "Ethical and Legal Issues in E-mail Therapy." In D. Bersoff (ed.), *Ethical Conflicts in Psychology*. Washington, D.C.: American Psychological Association, 2003.

Shea, P., and Armitage, S. *Guidelines for Creating Student Services On-line*. [www.wcet.info/projects/laap/guidelines]. 2002.

Shireman, R. "Ten Questions College Officials Should Ask About Diversity." *Chronicle of Higher Education Review*. August 15, 2003, p. B-10.

Shuman, W. *College for Sale: A Critique of the Commercialization of Higher Education*. Bristol, Pa.: Falmer Press, 1997.

Slaughter, S., and Leslie, L. L. *Academic Competition: Politics, Policies, and the Entre-preneurial Community*. Baltimore: Johns Hopkins University Press, 1997.

Smith, D. G., and Schonfeld, N. B. "The Benefits of Diversity: What the Research Tells Us." *About Campus*, 2000, 5 (4), 16–23.

Smith, P. *Killing the Spirit: Higher Education in America*. New York: Viking Penguin, 1990.

Sotto, R. "Technological Delivery Systems." In V. Gordon and W. Habley (eds.), *Academic Advising: A Comprehensive Handbook*. San Francisco: Jossey-Bass, 2003.

Sperling, J. *Rebel with a Cause: The Entrepreneur Who Created the University of Phoenix and the For-Profit Revolution in Higher Education*. New York: Wiley, 2000.

Stewart, D. L., and Peal, D. A. "In Practice: How We Can Improve Diversity Training." *About Campus*, 2001, 6 (4), 25–27.

Sue, D. W. *Counseling the Culturally Diverse: Theory and Practice*. (4th ed.) New York: Wiley, 2003.

Takaki, R. *A Different Mirror: A History of Multicultural America*. Boston: Little, Brown, 1993.

Talbot, D. M. "Masters Students' Perspectives on Their Graduate Education Regarding Issues of Diversity." *NASPA Journal*, 1999, 33, 163–178.

Talbot, M. *The Education of Women*. Chicago: University of Chicago Press, 1910.

Task Force of the National Advisory Council on Alcohol Abuse and Alco-holism. *A Call to Action: Changing the Culture of Drinking on U.S. Colleges*. Washington, D.C.: National Institute on Alcohol and Alcoholism, National Institutes of Health, 2002.

Terenzini, P. T. *Student Outcomes Information for Policy Making. Final Report on the National Postsecondary Education Cooperative Working Group on Student Outcomes from a Policy Perspective*. Washington, D.C.: U.S. Department of Education, Office of Research and Improvement, National Center for Educational Statistics, 1997.

Thelin, J. R. "Historical Overview of American Higher Education." In
    S. R. Komives, D. B. Woodard Jr., and Associates (eds.), *Student Services:
    A Handbook for the Profession*. (4th ed.) San Francisco: Jossey-Bass, 2003.

Tierney, W. G. "Native Voices in Academe: Strategies for Empowerment."
    Change, 1991, 23 (2), 36–44.

Tinto, V. *Leaving College: Rethinking the Causes and Cures of Student Attrition*.
    Chicago: University of Chicago Press, 1987.

Torres, V. "Mi Casa Is Not Exactly Like Your House." *About Campus*, 2003,
    8 (2), 2–7.

Torres, V. "The Diversity Among Us: Puerto Ricans, Cuban Americans,
    Caribbean Americans, and Central and South Americans." In
    A. M. Ortiz. (ed.), *Addressing the Unique Needs of Latino Students*. New
    Directions for Student Services, no. 105. San Francisco: Jossey-Bass,
    2004.

Torres, V., Howard-Hamilton, M., and Cooper, D. *Identity Development of Diverse
    Populations: Implications for Teaching and Administration in Higher Educa-
    tion*. ASHE-ERIC Higher Education Report. 29, No. 6, San Francisco:
    Jossey-Bass, 2003.

Trillin, C. *An Education in Georgia: Charlayne Hunter Gault and Hamilton
    Holmes: The Integration of the University of Georgia*. New York: Viking
    Penguin, 1964.

Trow, J. A. "Budgeting Climate." In D. B. Woodard Jr. (ed.), *Budgeting as a Tool
    for Policy in Student Affairs*. San Francisco: Jossey-Bass, 1995, p. 15.

Turnbull, W. W. "Are They Learning Anything in College?" *Change*, 1985,
    17 (6), 23–26.

Turner, C.S.V. (ed.). *Racial and Ethnic Diversity in Higher Education*. ASHE
    Reader Series. New York: Ginn Press, 1996.

Turrentine, C. G., and Conley, V. M. "Two Measures of Diversity Levels of the
    Labor Pool for Entry-level Student Affairs Positions." *NASPA Journal*,
    2001, 39 (1).

U.S. News & World Report. America's Best Colleges. U.S. News & World Report,
    2004.

Upcraft, M. L. "Assessment and Evaluation." In S. R. Komives and D. B.
    Woodard Jr. (eds.), *Student Services: A Handbook for the Profession*. (4th
    ed.) San Francisco: Jossey-Bass, 2003.

Upcraft, M. L., and Schuh, J. H. *Assessment in Student Affairs: A Guide for Practi-
    tioners*. San Francisco: Jossey-Bass, 1996.

Upcraft, M. L., and Schuh, J. H. *Assessment Practice in Student Affairs: An Applica-
    tions Manual*. San Francisco: Jossey-Bass, 2001.

Upcraft, M. L., and Stephens, D. S. "Academic Advising and Today's Changing Students." In V. N. Gardner, W. R. Habley, and R. H. Morales (eds.), *Academic Advising: A Comprehensive Handbook*. San Francisco: Jossey-Bass, 2000.

Vander Putten, J. "Bringing Social Class to the Diversity Challenge." *About Campus*, 2001, 6 (4), 14–19.

Vickery, L. J., and McClure, M. D. *The Four P's of Accessibility in Post-Secondary Education: Philosophy, Policies, Procedures and Programs*. Muncie, Ind.: Ball State University, 1998.

Walker, D. A., Reason, R. D., and Robinson, D. C. "Salary Predictors and Equity Issues for Administrators at Public and Private Institutions: From Dean to Director of Security." *NASPA Journal*, 2003, 40 (2).

Wall, V., and Evans, N. *Toward Acceptance: Sexual Orientation Issues on Campus*. Lanham, Md.: University Press of America, 1999.

Weber, M. *The Theory of Social and Economic Organization*. London: Oxford University Press, 1947.

White, L. "Deconstructing the Public-Private Dichotomy in Higher Education." *Change*, 2003, 35 (3), 46–54.

Whitt, E. J., and others. "Influences on Students' Openness to Diversity and Challenge in the Second and Third Years of College." *Journal of Higher Education*. 2001, 72, 172–204.

Wilder, D. J. *Seventeenth Annual Report on Minorities in Higher Education*. Washington, D.C.: American Council on Education, 2000.

Wilkinson, C. K., and Rund, J. A. "Supporting People, Programs and Structures for Diversity. In M. J. Barr, M. K. Desler, and Associates (eds.), *The Handbook for Student Affairs Administration*. (2nd ed.) San Francisco: Jossey-Bass, 2000.

Williamson, E. G. *Student Personnel Services in Colleges and Universities*. New York: McGraw-Hill, 1961.

Williamson, M. L., and Mamarchev, H. L. "A Systems Approach to Financial Management for Student Affairs." *NASPA Journal*, 1990, 27, p. 200.

Wilshire, B. W. *The Moral Collapse of the University: Professionalism, Purity, and Alienation*. Albany, N.Y.: State University of New York Press, 1990.

Wilson, R. "Educating for Diversity." *About Campus*, 1996, 1 (2), 4–9.

Wingspread Group on Higher Education. *An American Imperative: Higher Expectations for Higher Education*. Racine, Wis.: Johnson Foundation, 1993.

Wolff, R. A. *Incorporating Assessment into the Practice of Accreditation: A Preliminary Report*. Washington, D.C.: Council on Postsecondary Accreditation, 1992.

Woodard, D. B. "Finance and Budgeting." In R. B. Winston Jr., D. G. Creamer, and T. K. Miller (eds.), *The Professional Student Affairs Administrator: Educator, Leader, and Manager*. New York: Brunner/Mazel, 2001.

Woodard, D. B., and Komives, S. R. "Ensuring Staff Competence." In M. J. Barr and M. L. Upcraft (eds.), *New Futures for Student Affairs: Building a Vision for Professional Leadership and Practice*. San Francisco: Jossey-Bass, 1990.

Woodard, D. B., Love, P. G., and Komives, S. R. *Leadership and Management Issues for the New Century*. New Directions for Student Services, no. 92. San Francisco: Jossey-Bass, 2000.

Wrenn, G. C. *Student Personnel Work in College*. Somerset, N.J.: Ronald Press, 1951.

Wright, B., and Tierney, W. G. "American Indians in Higher Education: A History of Cultural Conflict." *Change*, 1991, *23* (2), 11–18.

Wright, D. J. (ed.). *Responding to the Needs of Today's Minority Students*. New Directions for Student Services, no. 38. San Francisco: Jossey-Bass, 1987.

Young, J. R. "Prozac Campus: More Students Seek Counseling and Take Psychiatric Medication." *Chronicle of Higher Education*, February 14, 2003.

Young, R. B. *No Neutral Ground: Standing By the Values We Prize in Higher Education*. San Francisco: Jossey-Bass, 1997.

Young, R. B. "Philosophies and Values Guiding the Student Affairs Profession." In S. R. Komives, D. B. Woodard Jr., and Associates (eds.), *Student Services: A Handbook for the Profession*. (4th ed.) San Francisco: Jossey-Bass, 2003.

Zachary, Lois J. *The Mentor's Guide: Facilitating Effective Learning Relationships*. San Francisco: Jossey-Bass, 2000.

Zemsky, R. "Have We Lost the 'Public' in Higher Education?" *Chronicle of Higher Education*. May 30, 2003.

Name Index

Subject Index

A

Academic advising, online, 111–113

Academic Counseling Expert (ACE) system, 112

Academic deans, reporting to, 45

Achieving Educational Excellence (Astin), 143

Addressing the Unique Needs of Latino American Students (Ortiz), 17

African-American students: and black male enrollment, 78–79; college adjustment of, 81–82; staff preparation for, 81; theoretical perspectives on, 14, 16–17

Alcohol and drug use: and college drinking statistics, 162; lack of effective approach to, 162–163

American Association for Higher Education (AAHE), 143

American Association of Community Colleges (AACC), 194

American College Personnel Association (ACPA), 8, 117, 129, 147, 163; and GLBT staff, 85; merger debate in, 194–195, 198; and needs of student affairs professionals, 191–192; overview of, 183, 186; and suggestions for collaborative/cooperative relationships, 193–194

American College Testing Program's Collegiate Assessment of Academic Proficiency (ACT) exam, 137

American College, The, (Sanford), 10–11

American Council on Education (ACE), 4, 5, 6, 34, 53, 54, 132, 195

American Counseling Association, 186–187

Americans with Disabilities Act, 84

Applying the Seven Principles for Good Practice in Undergraduate Education (Chickering and Gamson), 146

Asian-American students: enrollment growth of, 82; development model for, 17; and subpopulation differences, 83

Assessment, 135–142; changing role of, 138–139; and college rankings, 140; defined, 135; as dominant issue in higher education, 136–138; political and environmental impacts on, 141; progress in, 148; public demand for accountability and, 134; recent surveys and findings on, 139–141; regional accrediting associations and, 138; state legislatures and, 139